Beautiful Señoritas
& Other Plays

Dolores Prida

Edited and Introduced
by Judith Weiss

Arte Publico Press
Houston
Texas
1991

This volume is made possible through a grant from the National Endowment for the Arts, a federal agency.

Arte Publico Press
University of Houston
Houston, Texas 77204-2090

Cover Design by Mark Piñón

Beautiful señoritas & other plays / Dolores Prida.
p. cm.
English and Spanish.
Contents: Beautiful señoritas — Coser y cantar — Savings — Pantallas — Botánica.
ISBN 1-55885-026-0
1. Cuban Americans—Drama. I. Title. II. Title: Beautiful señoritas and other plays.
PS3566.R558B4 1990
812'.54–dc20 90-1239
CIP

The paper used in this publication meets the minimum requirements of the American National Standard for Permanence of Paper for Printed Library Materials Z39.48-1984. ♾

To Lola, my mother,
a seamstress whose life
was far from *coser y cantar*
but who, with inmense love
and patience hand-sewed
the seams of my life
with ever so careful and sturdy stitches
that have kept me whole
through much bending and stretching
through so much wear and tear
. . . so far from home . . .

Contents

"The Theaterworks of Dolores Prida," Judith Weiss . . 7
Beautiful Señoritas 17
Coser y cantar 47
Savings 69
Pantallas 117
Botánica 141

The Theaterworks of Dolores Prida

by

Prof. Judith Weiss
Mount Allison University
Sackville, N.B., Canada

The Theaterworks of Dolores Prida

Dolores Prida is ranked among the most important playwrights of the contemporary Hispanic theater in the United States. Prida belongs to a new generation of Latino women writing in North America: a hybrid generation, born in the Caribbean, Mexico or South America and raised in the United States; socially progressive yet still closely identified with their cultural roots. Her plays come as close to popular entertainment as plays can; their language, their characters, and the places have a comforting familiarity about them, and this commonness is made both emotionally liveable and artistically effective by skillful uses of humor, music, and references to texts of popular culture (from *santería* to soap operas, *boleros* to food).

These characteristics, the unique and the ordinary, are also suggested over and over again in Dolores Prida's own statements about herself and in what critics and reviewers have said about her. But there is no contradiction in seeing Prida as both a unique and a representative figure, once one realizes that everything about her career and her writings is a unique conjunction and expression of experiences common to millions of Hispanics in the United States.

Dolores Prida's career is somewhat out of the ordinary in that it has embraced virtually every field of the arts and letters: student (and college dropout), journalist, critic, scriptwriter for cinema and television, poet, theater director, administrator, editor of mass circulation magazines, translator, and publications director for the Association of Hispanic Arts. Her work has earned her a Doctor of Humane Letters degree from Mount Holyoke College (making her one of the few Latino writers to be awarded an honorary degree) and several awards and fellowships. Yet if the sum total of her activities and honors is unique, the individual endeavors are fairly typical for New York writers and Hispanic writers in the U.S. who build their creative careers as systematically as they can, while they navigate through financial uncertainty with an assortment of bread-and-butter assignments and jobs. Her multiple experiences are therefore fairly representative, but her versatility and her success are quite unusual, and Dolores Prida could well have been an invented paradigm of the Cuban-American woman writer in New York, a subspecies of the Latino artist and intellectual in North America.

The subjects of her plays are not unusual. On the contrary: she has always dealt with what comes most naturally to her as a Latino writer of her generation. What is unique is the breadth of subjects and their treatment. Prida experiments with a range of themes and of dramatic forms which place her work on the fine line between mainstream North American theater and Latin American popular theater, or on the edge between Off-Broadway theater and mass entertainment. The plays included in this collection also mark an evolution from a broad treatment of a variety of problems pertaining to Latino women, toward a more individualized focus for some of those same concerns. Over the twelve-year period represented by these five works (1978–1990), the author has not found any easy solution, but she has not tired, either, of airing the problems with humor, a dash of the cliché, and unfailing compassion.

Much of all this has to do with the ambiguity of Hispanic identity in the U.S. and with the ambivalence felt by the uprooted. The ambiguity is itself a dominant theme of her plays, because it remains the single most dominant theme of Hispanic life in the U.S. Five hundred years after the conquest of America, the process of transculturation is still very much alive, not so much, now, in the former colonies of Spain and Portugal as in the heart of the world power that has replaced Spain in this hemisphere. North-South, White-Black-Latino: it's in New York that one of the most dynamic meetings of races, languages and nationalities is now being felt and lived. The successive waves of Hispanic immigrants have become partially integrated into the system, making their mark on it, but they, in turn, are marked by the dominant culture and its values, and their own identity is almost always in question.

Add another factor: the individual ambivalence about being part of the "melting pot" but always the Other; the group tension that results from coexisting in increasingly congested spaces with other races, other linguistic groups, other cultures, and other nationalities. This coexistence is treated most lovingly (almost idealized) in *Savings*, a "musical fable," in which the cast of characters reads like a recipe for the Manhattan stew, and neighborhood institutions like the family-owned bank are a meeting-place for Puerto Rican, Cuban, Jewish, Black, and Italian New Yorkers.

There is the sense of never quite belonging, of being uprooted. Although most of Prida's characters are New Yorkers who consider Manhattan home, they are constantly confronted with the non-Hispanic's assumption that they are foreigners. And most of those who are immigrants are never quite cured of that feeling of not being entirely here. The distance from one's native land, carried within, can well up as a nostalgic memory or as an affirmation of what one still is in spite of the dominant culture. Or it can become a deliberate justification, enabling individuals to reject some of the less acceptable characteristics of their adopted country.

The characters of the most recent play, *Botánica*, struggle with this ambivalence. Millie (Milagros) has just graduated from an élite college in New Hampshire (where, in her words, she was able to study because it was her turn to be the token *spik* on scholarship). She returns to New York, but refuses at first to live in the same building as her mother and grandmother; she is going to work for the Chase Manhattan Bank and wants to leave the *barrio* behind. Her mother and grandmother, who run a medicinal herb shop, expect her to carry on the business. Millie eventually realizes that she cannot turn her back on them and finds a clever compromise, delegating the age-old information about traditional remedies to a computer's memory. The refrain of Pepe el Indio (a neighborhood street person), "Don't let them kill your buffaloes" fleshed out in Rubén's "When they kill our buffaloes, we'll be reduced to being tribes locked into reservations," inspires Millie's final response to the gentrification-real estate agent: "My buffaloes are not for sale."

The point of this conclusion is that her friend Rubén has persuaded her, by challenging her rejection of her background:

> What do you mean, "We're from here?" It's what we are: from here and from over there. That mixture. It's not how others see us or treat us. It's how we see ourselves, how we feel ... For me, "being from here" is, well ... it's mango and strawberries, alcapurrias and pretzels, Yemayá and the Yankees ... [...] Chase Manhattan and Changó. It all depends on how you pack your bags. [...] Out there there are plenty of people who think that even if you were born here and change your name to Millie or Joe—they think you're not from here anyway.

Hispanic women enjoy the advantage of individual freedom that North America affords them, but at the same time they are forced to deal with the traditional values which seek to impose themselves. For the more conservative elements in their families and communities, remaining attached to one's culture means accepting not only the authority of the collectivity over the individual, but also some of its most reactionary values, values which often conflict with the individualism and modern attitudes of North American society.

Hispanic artists and intellectuals are marked by the sign of commitment to a greater degree than their white North American counterparts. Like African American artists and intellectuals, even the Latinos who are most reluctant to acknowledge it feel a certain ethical and moral responsibility toward their community. In all Hispanic countries the artist and the intellectual have traditionally assumed the role of spokesperson, of conscience, or of critic, and historical tradition dies hard. In North America, the agent of the commercial media is a Mephistopheles for the committed artist and intellectual, offering rich resources and promising fame and fortune in exchange for the creator's soul (his or her values and commitment). This "crossover," as it is generally called, poses a particularly difficult dilemma for Latinos, as the price for artistic success can often be the watering-down of one's political expression, social consciousness, and group identity.

One net result of this alienation is well defined by the character ELLA, in *Coser y cantar*: "What the hell is emotional sophistication? Being like you? You, who don't even remember the smell of your own sweat, who can't recognize the sound of your own voice!"

Alienation of a different kind can pose a serious political problem within the Cuban community. If one is perceived as being too liberal or—heaven forbid—a radical, the personal situation of the artist and writer becomes quite complicated. The pressure from the right-wing Cuban exiles can be pitiless. When a group of young Cubans who were raised in the U.S. and Puerto Rico established a dialogue with the Cuban authorities in 1979, two were assassinated and others (including Dolores Prida) have been periodically subjected to death threats. And it is usually impossible for a Cuban artist or intellectual who falls into this category to present his or her works in "anti-Castro" territory (Miami, or parts of New Jersey), as a consequence of those threats. Because this has been part of Dolores Prida's personal experience it cannot be dismissed, even though it does not figure into these plays and Prida herself has continued to work professionally with artists and directors who are not sympathetic to the Cuban Revolution.

Class consciousness is also an important factor, albeit much stronger in the Hispanic immigrant community than among Anglos or second- or third-generation Hispanics, and within the Cuban exile community socioeconomic differences are not insignificant causes for discrimination, at least in the first generation. And the *déclassés*, white-collar employees or small shopkeepers, who after immigrating to the U.S. are forced to become manual workers, have a significant achievement to add to their psychological resumé.

The perspective of most of Prida's characters is that of the honest stiff, of the underdog, or of the socially responsible individual, and even when the characters are souls lost in a personal alienation (which is often the result of separation from the "body" of Latino culture), the play itself never surrenders to a jaded world view, to a nihilistic voice, or to existential despair. For all the humor of the treatment, moreover, the seriousness of the problems is always given its due; the author is basically earnest, and never flip or arrogant. When there is anger or bitterness, it is directed most often at the accomplices in the exploitation of their own people; the Latino yuppie in *Savings* and the males in *Beautiful Señoritas* are more easily savaged than the three aging soap opera stars of *Pantallas*, who clearly have a right to a more sympathetic treatment, as they play out their isolation in pathetic Pirandellian games after a lifetime of entertaining millions of television viewers.

If language, ethnicity, and social class form the conflicts and conjunctions in Dolores Prida's plays, her work is also characterized by a continual search for the appropriate idiom and dramatic structure. Prida is innovative in her eclectic search and in the twists with which she adapts a genre. Thus, a love of both the American musical and the strong Cuban-Spanish tradition of the musical comedy is variously expressed in the hilarious anti-machista satire of *Beautiful Señoritas* and in the deadly serious anti-gentrification protest of *Savings*; moreover, *Beautiful Señoritas* is built around a beauty pageant, another important form of mass entertainment which has been virtually impossible to uproot from Hispanic societies. The *Odd Couple*-cum-Woody Allen New York syndrome blends with lyric poetry, a dose of psychodrama, and music in *Coser y cantar*.

The *telenovela* (soap opera), which is probably the most popular form of mass entertainment in the Hispanic community, becomes the self-referential safety blanket of choice, with the coming of nuclear Armageddon in the dark satire *Pantallas*. With its Aristotelian structure and thematic development, *Botánica* falls squarely within the mainstream of Latin American and Latino theater and shows the influence of such perennial successes as René Marqués' *La carreta (The Oxcart)* and Francisco Arriví's *Vejigantes (Mummers)*.

The theatricality of Prida's works is most frequently accomplished through an integration of elements of popular culture (songs, proverbs, *santería* or mass culture—beauty pageants, soap operas) with a more conventional naturalism characteristic of the newer Latino drama (*Our Lady of the Tortilla, Union City Thanks-*

giving) and, of course, of the Latin American drama with the most popular appeal, from comedy to melodrama.

Sometimes, because of the fast-moving scenes, their tone, their characterization, and their language, the plays come to resemble the discourse of television. This is probably no coincidence, as it seems to signal quite clearly Prida's concern with discovering the optimal medium for reaching audiences, and it results in the creation of the ambiguous medium that is her theater.

The humor in Prida's works can be very revealing of the power of critical distance, the view of the semi-outsider. The most tender and subtle humor is reserved for relationships within the social group, be it the matrifocal family of *Botánica* or the close-knit community of *Savings*; it suggests the perspective of the insider standing outside the group and looking in on it with affection. On the other hand, it is the North American feminist rather than a culture-bound Latina who sets up the satire of *Beautiful Señoritas*, but only as a Latina could. The insider's knowledge of the music empowers her to turn it into a weapon against the dominant ideology, and Prida's response to attitudes about women's roles has a first-hand emotional familiarity about it. *Coser y cantar* is the comic confrontation of the two halves, with the humor exacerbated by the unlikely concentration of typical attitudes and behavior in each of the characters.

Pantallas offers a more complex expression of cultural duality. In its totality, the play is an exercise in gallows humor, a dark joke born out of the angst of the early eighties, when the Doomsday Clock was a universal theme of individual and social nightmares. *Pantallas* is reminiscent not only of Pirandello (with actors fixated on their roles and almost fixed in them) but also of Sartre's *No Exit* and of Beckett's *Endgame* and *Krapp's Last Tape*. The blank T.V. dominates the stage, like a replay of cartoons and jokes about the ultimate tragedy of nuclear war—not being able to watch T.V. because the power would go out. The fabric of the play, however, is made of the Spanish soap opera: lines and characters that most Hispanics will recognize in essence if not specifically, a mishmash of scripts that the three actors play as a parlor guessing game.

Pantallas, which addresses Spanish-speaking audiences in the U.S. and throughout Latin America, is premised upon an assumption of soap opera-literacy. Prida is not ridiculing the soaps, however, but poking gentle fun at them and at their veteran actors, much as she does with family. The main barb of the play thus lies not in its "inside" mode but on its global level of meaning; the gallows humor around nuclear annihilation underlies the tame, almost banal games played by the three characters, while the fragments of their scripts periodically make ironic allusions to the inconceivable destruction that is being unleashed outside their beach house.

Besides humor, language, and characters, certain key themes recur in Prida's works, often carrying a strong symbolic value. Chief among these is food. In *Coser y cantar*, the contrast between the fattening Caribbean foods favored by ELLA and the healthy foods promoted by SHE is a polarizing comic device. In *Savings*, an important manifestation of yuppy gentrification is the Tutti-Tofutti Health Restaurant and Bar, which invades the neighborhood along with a number of arts and crafts boutiques, while the *bodegas*, the groceries that sell Latin foods, have retreated well beyond the access of the residents or have simply disappeared. Thus, in *Savings*, yuppie food is not presented as the healthy rival of cholesterol-laden Caribbean cooking that it was in the earlier play, but rather as a malignant growth that displaces the old residents' source of nourishment.

In the first scene of *Botánica*, the *pasteles* that Millie's mother and grandmother are lovingly preparing for her graduation party are, for Millie, the concrete reason why she did not tell her family exactly when she was graduating. Those plantain and pork tamales would have been an invasion of the WASP space in which she had learned to survive by quietly denying her roots under peer pressure; the very smell of the *pasteles* would have thrown her back four years, when, as a frosh, she was first confronted by her classmates' racist prejudice. Rejecting the *pasteles* and keeping her family away from her college campus on graduation weekend means rejecting her grandmother's world, and Geno's collapse is due in part to that emotional rejection: the last words she utters before she faints are "La graduación, la graduación." And it is the grandmother's illness, for which Millie feels partly responsible, which leads her to follow in her footsteps as a wise woman. Food (the *pasteles*) is thus the first cause of the dramatic conflict.

From Pepe's obsession with the disappearing buffalo, one might extrapolate a concern about a vanishing food source that forms the basis of an entire culture. Thus, the now-mythical buffalo is a symbolic counterpart of the Caribbean *pasteles* and the play, which opened with Millie's symbolic rejection of her identity through the *pasteles*, concludes with her reaffirmation of ethnic loyalty through the buffalo reference. The Caribbean-American cultural duality becomes, in fact, the unity of identification of Latinos with the Native Americans, fellow-victims of the same territorial expansionists (the North American Anglo-Saxon Whites). This is indeed an interesting resolution to what had been a persistent dichotomy, and here, as in her other plays, the author reaffirms the importance of individual consciousness in saving the group identity and the strength that the individual continues to derive from community.

The recurrent themes in Dolores Prida's plays underscore the Latino paradox of a strong identity born of ambiguity. The works included in this collection trace a continuing struggle for self-definition. As she plays with a variety of schemes and formulas, the author progressively refines the process of integrating drama with other more dominant texts, mainly from Latino popular culture. This evolution parallels Prida's growth into maturity as a Latina writer and her broadened and strengthened self-definition as a Caribbean New Yorker.

Biographical note:

Judith A. Weiss (Ph.D., Yale), has published extensively on Latin American theater, literature and politics. Her book on the history of Latin American popular theater will be published shortly. Professor Weiss is on the faculty of Mount Allison University, in Canada, and she has also worked with Latino community theater in Washington, D.C.

Beautiful Señoritas

A Play with Music

1977

Beautiful Señoritas

CHARACTERS

Four BEAUTIFUL SEÑORITAS who also play assorted characters: Catch Women, Martyrs, Saints and just women.
The MIDWIFE, who also plays the Mother
The MAN, who plays all the male roles
The GIRL, who grows up before our eyes

SET

The set is an open space or a series of platforms and a ramp, which become the various playing areas as each scene flows into the next.

Beautiful Señoritas was first performed at Duo Theater in New York City on November 25, 1977 with the following cast:

THE BEAUTIFUL SEÑORITAS ..... Vira Colorado, María Norman Lourdes Ramírez and Lucy Vega
THE MIDWIFE .... Sol Echeverría
THE GIRL .... Viridiana Villaverde
THE MAN .... Manuel Yesckas

It was directed by Gloria Zelaya. Music by Tania León and Victoria Ruiz. Musical direction, Lydia Rivera. Choreography by Lourdes Ramírez.

Beautiful Señoritas opened on the West Coast April 6, 1979 at the Inner City Cultural Center's Stormy Weather Cafe in Los Angeles with the following cast:

THE BEAUTIFUL SEÑORITAS .... Roseanna Campos, Jeannie Linero Rosa María Márquez and Ilka Tanya Payán
THE MIDWIFE .... Peggy Hutcherson
THE GIRL .... Gabrielle Gazón
THE MAN .... Ron Godines

It was codirected by Eduardo Machado and Ilka Tanya Payán. Musical direction by Bob Zeigler. Choreography by Joanne Figueras.

ACT I

As lights go up DON JOSÉ *paces nervously back and forth. He smokes a big cigar, talking to himself.*

DON JOSÉ: Come on, woman. Hurry up. I have waited long enough for this child. Come on, a son. Give me a son ... I will start training him right away. To ride horses. To shoot. To drink. As soon as he is old enough I'll take him to La Casa de Luisa. There they'll teach him what to do to women. Ha, ha, ha! If he's anything like his father, in twenty years everyone in this town will be related to each other! Ha, ha, ha! My name will never die. My son will see to that ...

MIDWIFE: (MIDWIFE *enters running, excited.*) Don José! Don José!

DON JOSÉ: ¡Al fin! ¿Qué? Dígame, ¿todo está bien?

MIDWIFE: Yes, everything is fine, Don José. Your wife just gave birth to a healthy ...

DON JOSÉ: (*Interrupting excitedly*). Ha, ha, I knew it! A healthy son!

MIDWIFE: ... It is a girl Don José ...

DON JOSÉ: (*Disappointment and disbelief creep onto his face. Then anger. He throws the cigar on the floor with force, then steps on it.*) A girl! ¡No puede ser! ¡Imposible! What do you mean a girl! ¡Cómo puede pasarme esto a mí? The first child that will bear my name and it is a ... girl! ¡Una chancleta! ¡Carajo! (*He storms away, muttering under his breath.*)

MIDWIFE: (*Looks at* DON JOSÉ *as he exits, then addresses the audience. At some point during the following monologue the Girl will appear. She looks at everything as if seeing the world for the first time.*) He's off to drown his disappointment in rum, because another woman is born into this world. The same woman another man's son will covet and pursue and try to rape at the first opportunity. The same woman whose virginity he will protect with a gun. Another woman is born into this world. In Managua, in San Juan, in an Andes mountain town. She'll be put on a pedestal and trampled upon at the same time. She will be made a saint and a whore, crowned queen and exploited and adored. No, she's not just any woman. She will be called upon to ... (*The* MIDWIFE *is interrupted by off-stage voices.*)

BEAUTIFUL SEÑORITA 1: ¡Cuchi cuchi chi-a-boom!
BEAUTIFUL SEÑORITA 2: ¡Mira caramba oye!
BEAUTIFUL SEÑORITA 3: ¡Rumba pachanga mambo!
BEAUTIFUL SEÑORITA 4: ¡Oye papito, ay ayayaiiii!

Immediately a rumba is heard. The four BEAUTIFUL SEÑORITAS *enter dancing. They dress as Carmen Miranda, Iris Chacón, Charo and María la O. They sing:*

"THE BEAUTIFUL SEÑORITAS SONG"

WE BEAUTIFUL SEÑORITAS
WITH MARACAS IN OUR SOULS
MIRA PAPI AY CARIÑO
ALWAYS READY FOR AMOR

WE BEAUTIFUL SEÑORITAS
MUCHA SALSA AND SABOR
CUCHI CUCHI LATIN BOMBAS
ALWAYS READY FOR AMOR

AY CARAMBA MIRA OYE
DANCE THE TANGO ALL NIGHT LONG
GUACAMOLE LATIN LOVER
ALWAYS READY FOR AMOR

ONE PAPAYA ONE BANANA
AY SÍ SÍ SÍ SÍ SEÑOR
SIMPÁTICAS MUCHACHITAS
ALWAYS READY FOR AMOR

PIÑA PLÁTANOS CHIQUITAS
OF THE RAINBOW EL COLOR
CUCARACHAS MUY BONITAS
ALWAYS READY FOR AMOR

WE BEAUTIFUL SEÑORITAS
WITH MARACAS IN OUR SOULS
MIRA PAPI AY CARIÑO
ALWAYS READY FOR AMOR

AY SÍ SÍ SÍ SÍ SEÑOR
ALWAYS READY FOR AMOR
AY SÍ SÍ SÍ SÍ SEÑOR
ALWAYS READY FOR AMOR
¡AY SÍ SÍ SÍ SÍ SEÑOR!

The SEÑORITAS *bow and exit.* MARÍA LA O *returns and takes more bows.*

MARÍA LA O *bows for the last time. Goes to her dressing room. Sits down and removes her shoes.*

MARÍA LA O: My feet are killing me. These juanetes get worse by the minute. (*She rubs her feet. She appears older and tired, all the glamour gone out of her. She takes her false eye lashes off, examines her face carefully in the mirror, begins to remove makeup.*) Forty lousy bucks a week for all that tit-shaking. But I need the extra money. What am I going to do? A job is a job. And with my artistic inclinations ... well ... But look at this joint! A dressing room! They have the nerve to call this a dressing room. I have to be careful not to step on a rat. They squeak too loud. The patrons out there may hear, you know. Anyway, I sort of liked dancing since I was a kid. But this! I meant dancing like Alicia Alonso, Margot Fonteyn ... and I end up as a cheap Iris Chacón. At least she shook her behind in Radio City Music Hall. Ha! That's one up the Rockettes!

BEAUTY QUEEN: (*She enters, wearing a beauty contest bathing suit.*) María la O, you still here. I thought everyone was gone. You always run out after the show.

MARÍA LA O. No, not tonight. Somebody is taking care of the kid. I'm so tired that I don't feel like moving from here. Estoy muerta, m'ija. (*Looks* BEAUTY QUEEN *up and down.*) And where are *you* going?

BEAUTY QUEEN: To a beauty contest, of course.

MARÍA LA O: Don't you get tired of that, mujer!

BEAUTY QUEEN: Never. I was born to be a beauty queen. I have been a beauty queen ever since I was born. "La reinecita," they used to call me. My mother entered me in my first contest at the age of two. Then, it was one contest after the other. I have been in a bathing suit ever since. I save a lot in clothes ... Anyway, my mother used to read all those womens magazines—*Vanidades*, *Cosmopolitan*,

Claudia, Buenhogar—where everyone is so beautiful and happy. She, of course, wanted me to be like them ... (*Examines herself in the mirror.*) I have won hundreds of contests, you know. I have been Queen of Los Hijos Ausentes Club; Reina El Diario-La Prensa; Queen of Plátano Chips; Queen of the Hispanic Hairdressers Association; Reina de la Alcapurria; Miss Caribbean Sunshine; Señorita Turismo de Staten Island; Queen of the Texas Enchilada ... and now of course, I am Miss Banana Republic!

MARÍA LA O: Muchacha, I bet you don't have time for anything else!

BEAUTY QUEEN: Oh, I sure do. I wax my legs every day. I keep in shape. I practice my smile. Because one day, in one of those beauty contests, someone will come up to me and say ...

MARÍA LA O: You're on Candid Camera?

BEAUTY QUEEN: ... Where have you been all my life! I'll be discovered, become a movie star, a millionaire, appear on the cover of *People Magazine* ... and anyway, even if I don't win, I still make some money.

MARÍA LA O: Money? How much money?

BEAUTY QUEEN: Five hundred. A thousand. A trip here. A trip there. Depends on the contest.

MARÍA LA O: I could sure use some extra chavos ... Hey, do you think I could win, be discovered by a movie producer or something ...

BEAUTY QUEEN: Weeell ... I don't know. They've just re-made "King Kong" ... ha, ha!

MARÍA LA O: (MARÍA LA O *doesn't pay attention. She's busily thinking about the money.* BEAUTY QUEEN *turns to go.*) Even if I am only third, I still make some extra money. I can send Johnny home for the summer. He's never seen his grandparents. Ya ni habla español. (MARÍA LA O *quickly tries to put eye lashes back on. Grabs her shoes and runs after* BEAUTY QUEEN.) Wait, wait for me! ¡Espérame! I'll go with you to the beauty contest! (*She exits. The* MIDWIFE *enters immediately. She calls after* MARÍA LA O.)

MIDWIFE: And don't forget to smile! Give them your brightest smile! As if your life depended on it!

The GIRL *enters and sits at* MARÍA LA O'*s dressing table. During the following monologue, the* GIRL *will play with the makeup, slowly applying lipstick, mascara, and eye shadow in a very serious, concentrated manner.*

MIDWIFE: Yes. You have to smile to win. A girl with a serious face has no future. But what can you do when a butterfly is trapped in your insides and you cannot smile? How can you smile with a butterfly condemned to beat its ever-changing wings in the pit of your stomach? There it is. Now a flutter. Now a storm. Carried by the winds of emotion, this butterfly transforms the shape, the color, the texture of its wings; the speed and range of its flight. Now it becomes a stained glass butterfly, light shining through its yellow-colored wings, which move ever so slowly, up and down, up and down, sometimes remaining still for a second too long. Then the world stops and takes a plunge, becoming a brief black hole in space. A burned-out star wandering through the galaxies is like a smile meant, but not delivered. And I am so full of undelivered smiles! So pregnant with undetected laughter! Sonrisas, sonrisas, who would exchange a butterfly for a permanent smile! Hear, hear, this butterfly will keep you alive and running, awake and on your toes, speeding along the herd of wild horses stampeding through the heart! This butterfly is magic. It changes its size. It becomes big and small. Who will take this wondrous butterfly and give me a simple, lasting smile! A smile for day and night, winter and fall. A smile for all ocassions. A smile to survive . . . (*With the last line, the* MIDWIFE *turns to the* GIRL, *who by now has her face made up like a clown. They look at each other. The* GIRL *faces the audience. She is not smiling. They freeze. Black out.*)

In the dark we hear a fanfare. Lights go up on the MC. He wears a velvet tuxedo with a pink ruffled shirt. He combs his hair, twirls his moustache, adjusts his bow tie and smiles. He wields a microphone with a flourish.

MC: Ladies and gentlemen. Señoras y señores. Tonight. Esta noche. Right here. Aquí mismo. You will have the opportunity to see the most exquisite, sexy, exotic, sandungueras, jacarandosas and most beautiful señoritas of all. You will be the judge of the contest, where beauty will compete with belleza; where women of the tropical Caribbean will battle the señoritas of South America. Ladies and gentlemen, the poets have said it. The composers of boleros have said it. Latin women are the most beautiful, the most passionate, the most virtuous, the best housewives and cooks. And they all know how to dance to salsa, and do the hustle, the mambo, the guaguancó ... And they are always ready for amor, señores! What treasures! See for yourselves! ... Ladies and gentlemen, señoras y señores ... from the sandy beaches of Florida, esbelta as a palm tree, please welcome Miss Little Havana! (*Music from "Cuando salí de Cuba" is heard. Miss Little Havana enters. She wears a bathing suit, sun glasses and a string of pearls. She sings.*)

CUANDO SALÍ DE CUBA
DEJÉ MI CASA, DEJÉ MI AVIÓN
CUANDO SALÍ DE CUBA
DEJÉ ENTERRADO MEDIO MILLÓN

MC: Oye, chica, what's your name?

MISS LITTLE HAVANA: Fina de la Garza del Vedado y Miramar. From the best families of the Cuba de Ayer.

MC: (*To the audience.*) As you can see, ladies and gentlemen, Fina es muy fina. Really fine, he, he, he. Tell the judges, Fina, what are your best assets?

MISS LITTLE HAVANA: Well, back in the Cuba of Yesterday, I had a house with ten rooms and fifty maids, two cars, un avión and a sugar mill. But Fidel took everything away. So, here in the U.S. of A. my only assets are 36-28-42.

MC: Hmmm! That's what I call a positive attitude. Miss Fina, some day you'll get it all back. Un aplauso for Fina, ladies and gentlemen! (MISS LITTLE HAVANA *steps back and freezes into a doll-like posture, with a fixed smile on her face.*)

MC: Now, from South of the Border, ladies and gentlemen—hold on to your tacos, because here she is ... Miss Chili Tamale! (*Music begins: "Allá en el Rancho Grande".*) Please, un aplauso! Welcome, welcome chaparrita! (MISS CHILI TAMALE *enters. She also wears a bathing suit and a sarape over her shoulder. She sings.*)

ALLÁ EN EL RANCHO GRANDE
ALLA DONDE VIVÍA
YO ERA UNA FLACA MORENITA
QUE TRISTE SE QUEJABA
QUE TRISTE SE QUEJAABAAA
NO TENGO NI UN PAR DE CALZONES

NI SIN REMIENDOS DE CUERO
NI DOS HUEVOS RANCHEROS
Y LAS TORTILLAS QUEMADAS

MC: Your name, beautiful señorita?

MISS CHILI TAMALE: Lupe Lupita Guadalupe Viva Zapata y Enchilada, para servirle.

MC: What good manners! Tell us, what's your most fervent desire?

MISS CHILI TAMALE: My most fervent desire is to marry a big, handsome, very rich americano.

MC: Aha! What have we here! You mean you prefer gringos instead of Latin men?

MISS CHILI TAMALE: Oh no, no no. But, you see, I need my green card. La migra is after me.

MC: (*Nervously, the* MC *looks around, then pushes* MISS TAMALE *back. She joins* MISS LITTLE HAVANA *in her doll-like pose.*) Ahem, ahem. Now, ladies and gentlemen, the dream girl of every American male, the most beautiful señorita of all. Created by Madison Avenue exclusively for the United Fruit Company ... ladies and gentlemen, please welcome Miss Conchita Banana! (*"Chiquita Banana" music begins.* MISS CONCHITA BANANA *enters. She wears plastic bananas on her head and holds two real ones in her hands. She sings.*)

I'M CONCHITA BANANA
AND I'M HERE TO SAY
THAT BANANAS TASTE THE BEST
IN A CERTAIN WAY
YOU CAN PUT'EM IN YOUR HUM HUM
YOU CAN SLICE'EM IN YOUR HA HA
ANYWAY YOU WANT TO EAT'EM
ITS IMPOSSIBLE TO BEAT'EM
BUT NEVER, NEVER, NEVER
PUT BANANAS IN THE REFRIGERATOR
NO, NO, NO NO!

(*She throws the two real bananas to the audience.*)

MC: Brava, bravissima, Miss Banana! Do you realize you have made our humble fruit, el plátano, very very famous all over the world?

MISS CONCHITA BANANA: Yes, I know. That has been the goal of my whole life.

MC: And we are proud of you, Conchita. But, come here, just between the two of us . . . tell me the truth, do you really like bananas?

MISS CONCHITA BANANA: Of course, I do! I eat them all the time. My motto is: a banana a day keeps the doctor away!

MC: (*Motioning to audience to applaud.*) What intelligence! What insight! Un aplauso, ladies and gentlemen . . . (MISS CONCHITA BANANA *bows and steps back, joining the other doll-like contestants. As each woman says the following lines she becomes human again. The MC moves to one side and freezes.*)

WOMAN 1 (*Previously* MISS LITTLE HAVANA.) No one knows me. They see me passing by, but they don't know me. They don't see me. They hear my accent but not my words. If anyone wants to find me, I'll be sitting by the beach.

WOMAN 2 (*Previously* MISS CHILI TAMALE.) My mother, my grandmother, and her mother before her, walked the land with barefeet, as I have done too. We have given birth to our daughters on the bare soil. We have seen them grow and go to market. Now we need permits to walk the land—our land.

WOMAN 3 (*Previously* MISS CONCHITA BANANA.) I have been invented for a photograph. Sometimes I wish to be a person, to exist for my own sake, to stop dancing, to stop smiling. One day I think I will want to cry.

MC: (*We hear a fanfare. The* MC *unfreezes. The contestants become dolls again.*) Ladies and gentlemen . . . don't go away, because we still have more for you! Now, señoras y señores, from la Isla del Encanto, please welcome Miss Commonwealth! Un aplauso, please! (*We hear music from "Cortaron a Elena."* MISS COMMONWEALTH *enters, giggling and waving. She sings.*)

CORTARON EL BUDGET
CORTARON EL BUDGET
CORTARON EL BUDGET
Y NOS QUEDAMOS
SIN FOOD STAMPS
CORTARON A ELENA
CORTARON A JUANA
CORTARON A LOLA
Y NOS QUEDAMOS

SIN NA' PA' NA'

MC: ¡Qué sabor! Tell us your name, beautiful jibarita ...
MISS COMMONWEALTH: Lucy Wisteria Rivera (*Giggles.*)
MC: Let me ask you, what do you think of the political status of the island?
MISS COMMONWEALTH: (*Giggles.*) Oh, I don't know about that. La belleza y la política no se mezclan. Beauty and politics do not mix. (*Giggles.*)
MC: True, true, preciosa-por-ser-un-encanto-por-ser-un-edén. Tell me, what is your goal in life?
MISS COMMONWEALTH: I want to find a boyfriend and get married. I will be a great housewife, cook and mother. I will only live for my husband and my children. (*Giggles.*)
MC: Ave María, nena! You are a tesoro! Well, Miss Commonwealth, finding a boyfriend should not be difficult for you. You have everything a man wants right there up front. (*Points to her breasts with the microphone.*) I am sure you already have several novios, no?
MISS COMMONWEALTH: Oh no, I don't have a boyfriend yet. My father doesn't let me. And besides, it isn't as easy as you think. To catch a man you must know the rules of the game, the technique, the tricks, the know-how, the how-to, the expertise, the go-get-it, the ... works! Let me show you. (*The* MC *stands to one side and freezes. The doll-like contestants in the back exit.* MISS COMMONWEALTH *begins to exit. She runs into the* GIRL *as she enters.* MISS COMMONWEALTH'*s crown falls to the floor. She looks at the girl who seems to remind her of something far away.*)
WOMAN 4: (*Previously* MISS COMMONWEALTH.) The girl who had never seen the ocean decided one day to see it. Just one startled footprint on the sand and the sea came roaring at her. A thousand waves, an infinite horizon, a storm of salt and two diving birds thrusted themselves furiously into her eyes. Today she walks blindly through the smog and the dust of cities and villages. But she travels with a smile, because she carries the ocean in her eyes. (WOMAN 4 *exits. Spot on the* GIRL. *She picks up the crown from the floor and places it on her head. Spot closes in on the crown.*)

As lights go up, the MAN *enters with a chair and places it center stage. He sits on it. The* GIRL *sits on the floor with her back to the audience. The* CATCH WOMEN *enter and take their places around the man. Each* WOMAN *addresses the* GIRL, *as a teacher would.*)

CATCH WOMAN 1: There are many ways to catch a man. Watch ... (*Walks over to the* MAN.) Hypnotize him. Be a good listener. (*She sits on his knees.*) Laugh at his jokes, even if you heard them before. (*To* MAN.) Honey, tell them the one about the two bartenders ... (*The* MAN *mouths words as if telling a joke. She listens and laughs loudly. Gets up.*) Cuá, cuá, cuá! Isn't he a riot! (*She begins to walk away, turns and addresses the* GIRL.) Ah, and don't forget to move your hips.

CATCH WOMAN 2: (CATCH WOMAN 1 *walks moving her hips back to her place.* CATCH WOMAN 2 *steps forward and addresses the* GIRL.) Women can't be too intellectual. He will get bored. (*To* MAN, *in earnest.*) Honey, don't you think nuclear disarmament is our only hope for survival? (*The* MAN *yawns. To* GIRL.) See? When a man goes out with a woman he wants to relax, to have fun, to feel good. He doesn't want to talk about heavy stuff, know what I mean? (CATCH WOMAN 2 *walks back to her place. She flirts with her boa, wrapping it around the man's head. Teasing.*) Toro, toro, torito!

CATCH WOMAN 3: (*The* MAN *charges after* CATCH WOMAN 2. CATCH WOMAN 3 *stops him with a hypnotic look. He sits down again.* CATCH WOMAN 3 *addresses the* GIRL.) Looks are a very powerful weapon. Use your eyes, honey. Look at him now and then. Directly. Sideways. Through your eyelashes. From the corner of your eyes. Over your sunglasses. Look at him up and down. But not with too much insistence. And never ever look directly at his crotch. (*She walks away dropping a handkerchief. The* MAN *stops to pick it up.* CATCH WOMAN 4 *places her foot on it. Pushes the* MAN *away.*) Make him suffer. Make him jealous. (*Waves to someone offstage, flirting.*) Hi Johnny! (*To* GIRL.) They like it. It gives them a good excuse to get drunk. Tease him. Find out what he likes. (*To* MAN.) Un masajito, papi? I'll make you a burrito de machaca con huevo, sí? (*She massages his neck.*) Keep him in suspense. (*To* MAN.) I love you. I don't love you. Te quiero. No te quiero. I love you. I don't love you ... (*She walks away.*)

ALL: (*All four* CATCH WOMEN *come forward.*) We do it all for him!

MAN: They do it all for me! (MAN *raps the song, while the* CATCH WOMEN *parade around him.*)

"THEY DO IT ALL FOR ME"

(*Wolf whistles.*)
MIRA MAMI, PSST, COSA LINDA!
OYE MUÑECA, DAME UN POQUITO
AY, MIREN ESO
LO QUE DIOS HA HECHO
PARA NOSOTROS LOS PECADORES
AY MAMÁ, DON'T WALK LIKE THAT
DON'T MOVE LIKE THAT
DON'T LOOK LIKE THAT
'CAUSE YOU GONNA GIVE ME
A HEART ATTACK
THEY DO IT ALL FOR ME
WHAT THEY LEARN IN A MAGAZINE
THEY DO IT ALL FOR ME
'CAUSE YOU KNOW WHAT THEY WANT
AY MAMÁ, TAN PRECIOSA TAN HERMOSA
GIVE ME A PIECE OF THIS
AND A PIECE OF THAT
'CAUSE I KNOW YOU DO IT ALL FOR ME
DON'T YOU DON'T YOU
DON'T YOU DO IT ALL FOR ME

(CATCH WOMAN 2 *throws her boa around his neck, ropes in the* MAN *and exits with him in tow.*)

CATCH WOMAN 1: ¡Mira, esa mosquita muerta ya agarró uno!

CATCH WOMAN 3: Look at that, she caught him!

CATCH WOMAN 4: Pero, ¡qué tiene ella que no tenga yo! (*All exit. The* GIRL *stands up, picks up the handkerchief from the floor. Mimes imitations of some of the* WOMEN'*s moves, flirting, listening to jokes, giggling, moving her hips, etc. Church music comes on.*

The NUN *enters carrying a bouquet of roses cradled in her arms. She stands in the back and looks up bathed in a sacred light. Her lips move as if praying. She lowers her eyes and sees the* GIRL *imitating more sexy moves. The* NUN'*s eyes widen in disbelief.*

NUN: What are you doing, creature? That is sinful! A woman must be recatada, saintly. Thoughts of the flesh must be banished from your head and your heart. Close your eyes and your pores to desire. The only love there is is the love of the Lord. The Lord is the only lover!

NUN: (*The* GIRL *stops, thoroughly confused. The* NUN *strikes her with the bouquet of roses.*) ¡Arrodíllate! Kneel down on these roses! Let your blood erase your sinful thoughts! You may still be saved. Pray, pray! (*The* GIRL *kneels on the roses, grimacing with pain. The* PRIEST *enters, makes the sign of the cross on the scene. The* NUN *kneels in front of the* PRIEST.) Father, forgive me for I have sinned ... (*The* SEÑORITAS *enter with her lines. They wear mantillas and peinetas, holding Spanish fans in their hands, a red carnation between their teeth.*)

SEÑORITA 1: Me too, father!

SEÑORITA 2: ¡Y yo también!

SEÑORITA 3: And me!

SEÑORITA 4: Me too! (*A tango begins. The following lines are integrated into the choreography.*)

SEÑORITA 1: Father, it has been two weeks since my last confession ...

PRIEST: Speak, hija mia.

SEÑORITA 2: Padre, my boyfriend used to kiss me on the lips ... but it's all over now ...

PRIEST: Lord, oh Lord!

SEÑORITA 3: Forgive me father, but I have masturbated three times. Twice mentally, once physically.

PRIEST: Ave María Purísima sin pecado concebida ...

SEÑORITA 4: I have sinned, santo padre. Last night I had wet dreams.

PRIEST: Socorro espiritual, Dios mío. Help these lost souls!

SEÑORITA 1: He said, fellatio ... I said, cunnilingus!

PRIEST: No, not in a beautiful señorita's mouth! Such evil words, Señor, oh Lord!

SEÑORITA 2: Father, listen. I have sinned. I have really really sinned. I did it, I did it! All the way I did it! (*All the* SEÑORITAS *and the* NUN *turn to* SEÑORITA 2 *and make the sign of the cross. They point at her with the fans.*)

SEÑORITAS 1, 3, 4: She's done it, Dios mío, she's done it! Santísima Virgen, she's done it!

PRIEST: She's done it! She's done it!

SEÑORITA 2: (*Tangoing backwards.*) I did it. yes. Lo hice. I did it, father. Forgive me, for I have fornicated!

PRIEST: She's done it! She's done it! (*The* NUN *faints in the* PRIEST'*s arms.*)

SEÑORITAS 1, 3, 4: Fornication! Copulation! Indigestion! ¡Qué pecado y que horror! ¡Culpable! ¡Culpable! ¡Culpable! (*They exit tangoing. The* PRIEST, *with the fainted* NUN *in his arms looks at the audience bewildered.*)

PRIEST: (*To audience.*) Intermission! *Black out*

ACT II

In the dark we hear a fanfare. Spot light on MC.

MC: Welcome back, ladies and gentlemen, señoras y señores. There's more, much much more yet to come. For, you see, our contestants are not only beautiful, but also very talented señoritas. For the benefit of the judges they will sing, they will dance, they will perform the most daring acts on the flying trapeze!

Spot light on WOMAN 3 *swinging on a swing center stage. She sings:*

"BOLERO TRAICIONERO"

TAKE ME IN YOUR ARMS
LET'S DANCE AWAY THE NIGHT
WHISPER IN MY EARS
THE SWEETEST WORDS OF LOVE

I'M THE WOMAN IN YOUR LIFE
SAY YOU DIE EVERY TIME
YOU ARE AWAY FROM ME
AND WHISPER IN MY EAR
THE SWEETEST WORDS OF LOVE

PROMISE ME THE SKY
GET ME THE MOON, THE STARS
IF IT IS A LIE
WHISPER IN MY EAR
THE SWEETEST WORDS OF LOVE

DARLING IN A DREAM OF FLOWERS

WE ARE PLAYING ALL THE GREATEST GAMES
LIE TO ME WITH ROMANCE AGAIN
TRAICIÓNAME ASÍ, TRAICIÓNAME MÁS

(Bis)
PROMISE ME THE SKY . . .

(*During the song lights go up to reveal the other women sitting in various poses waiting to be asked to dance. The* GIRL *is also there, closely watched by the* CHAPERONE, *who also keeps an eye on all the other women. The* MAN *enters wearing a white tuxedo and a Zorro mask. He dances with each one. Gives each a flower, which he pulls out of his pocket like a magician. The* GIRL *wants to dance, the* MAN *comes and asks her, but the* CHAPERONE *doesn't let her. The* MAN *asks another woman to dance. They dance very close. The* CHAPERONE *comes and taps the woman on the shoulder. They stop dancing. The* MAN *goes to the woman singing, pushes the swing back and forth. At the end of the song, the singer leaves with the* MAN. *The other women follow them with their eyes.*)

SEÑORITA 2: I swear I only did it for love! He sang in my ear the sweetest words, the most romantic boleros. Saturdays and Sundays he sat at the bar across the street drinking beer. He kept playing the same record on the juke box over and over. It was a pasodoble about being as lonely as a stray dog. He would send me flowers and candies with the shoeshine boy. My father and brother had sworn to kill him if they saw him near me. But he insisted. He kept saying how much he loved me and he kept getting drunk right at my doorsteps. He serenaded me every weekend. He said I was the most decent woman in the world. Only his mother was more saintly . . . he said.

SEÑORITA 3: He said the same thing to me. Then he said the same thing to my sister and then to her best friend. My sister was heartbroken. She was so young. She had given him her virginity and he would not marry her. Then three days before Christmas she set herself on fire. She poured gasoline on her dress, put a match to it and then started to run. She ran like a vision of hell through the streets of the town. Her screams awoke all the dead lovers for miles around. Her long hair, her flowing dress were like a banner of fire calling followers to battle. She ran down Main Street—the street that leads directly to the sea. I ran after her trying to catch her to embrace her, to smother the flames with my own body. I ran after her, yelling not to go into the water. She couldn't, she wouldn't hear. She ran into the sea like thunder ... Such drama, such fiery spectacle, such pain ... It all ended with a half-silent hiss and a thin column of smoke rising up from the water, near the beach where we played as children ... (*We hear the sound of drums. The women join in making mournful sounds.*)

The mournful sounds slowly turn into the "Wedding Song."

"THE WEDDING SONG"
("Where Have All the Women Gone")

WOMAN:
THERE, THERE'S JUANA
SEE JUANA JUMP
SEE HOW SHE JUMPS
WHEN HE DOES CALL
THERE, THERE'S ROSA
SEE ROSA CRY
SEE HOW SHE CRIES
WHEN HE DOESN'T CALL

CHORUS:
WHERE HAVE ALL
THE WOMEN GONE

WOMAN:
JUANA ROSA CARMEN GO
NOT WITH A BANG
BUT WITH A WHIMPER
WHERE HAVE THEY GONE
LEAVING THEIR DREAMS
BEHIND
LEAVING THEIR DREAMS
LETTING THEIR LIVES
UNDONE

CHORUS:
(Wedding March Music.)
LOOK HOW THEY GO
LOOK AT THEM GO

SIGHING AND CRYING
LOOK AT THEM GO

Towards the end of the song the women will form a line before the CHAPERONE *who is holding a big basket. From it she takes and gives each woman a wig with hairrollers on it. Assisted by the* GIRL, *each woman will put her wig on. Once the song ends, each woman will start miming various housecleaning chores: sweeping, ironing, washing, etc. The* MOTHER *sews. The* GIRL *watches.*

MARTYR 1: Cry my child. Las mujeres nacimos para sufrir. There's no other way but to cry. One is born awake and crying. That's the way God meant it. And who are we to question the ways of the Lord?

MARTYR 2: I don't live for myself. I live for my husband and my children. A woman's work is never done: what to make for lunch, cook the beans, start the rice, and then again, what to make for supper, and the fact that Juanito needs new shoes for school. (*She holds her side in pain.*)

MARTYR 3: What's wrong with you?

MARTYR 2: I have female problems.

MARTYR 3: The menstruation again?

MARTYR 2: No, my husband beat me up again last night. (*The* GIRL *covers her ears, then covers her eyes and begins to play "Put the Tail on the Donkey" all by herself.*)

MARTYR 3: I know what you mean, m'ija. We women were born to suffer. I sacrifice myself for my children. But, do they appreciate it? No. Someday, someday when I'm gone they'll remember me and all I did for them. But then it will be too late. Too late.

MOTHER: Such metaphysics. Women should not worry about philosophical matters. That's for men. (*She returns to her sewing, humming a song of oblivion.*)

MARTYR 3: The Virgin Mary never worried about forced sterilization or torture in Argentina or minimum wages. True, she had housing problems, but I'm sure there was never a quarrel as to who washed the dishes or fed that burro.

MAMA: Such heretic thoughts will not lead to anything good, I tell you. It is better not to have many thoughts. When you do the ironing or the cooking or set your hair in rollers, it is better not to think too much. I know what I'm saying. I know ... (*Continues her sewing and humming.*)

MARTYR 1: And this headache. We're born with migraine. And with the nerves on edge. It is so, I know. I remember my mother and her mother before her. They always had jaquecas. I inherited the pain and tazas de tilo, the Valiums and the Libriums ...

MAMA: You don't keep busy enough. While your hands are busy ...

MARTYR 2: ... And your mouth is busy, while you run from bed to stove to shop to work to sink to bed to mirror no one notices the little light shining in your eyes. It is better that way ... because I ... I don't live for myself. I live for my husband and my children, and it is better that they don't notice that flash in my eyes, that sparkle of a threat, that flickering death wish ... (*The* GIRL *tears off the cloth covering her eyes. Looks at the women expecting some action. Mumbling and complaining under their breaths, the women go back to their chores. The* GUERRILLERA *enters. She is self-assured and full of energy. The* GIRL *gives her all her attention.*)

GUERRILLERA: Stop your laments, sisters!

MARTYR 1: Who's she?

GUERRILLERA: Complaining and whining won't help!

MARTYR 3: That's true!

GUERRILLERA: We can change the world and then our lot will improve!

MARTYR 3: It's about time!

GUERRILLERA: Let's fight oppresion!

MARTYR 3: I'm ready! Let's go!

MARTYR 2: I ain't going nowhere. I think she's a lesbian.

GUERRILLERA: We, as third world women ...

MARTYR 1: Third world ... ? I'm from Michoacán ...

GUERRILLERA: ... Are triply oppressed, so we have to fight three times as hard!

MARTYR 3: That's right!

GUERRILLERA: Come to the meetings!

MARTYR 3: Where? Where? When?

GUERRILLERA: ... Have your consciousness raised!

MARTYR 2: What's consciousness?

MARTYR 1: I don't know, but I'm keeping my legs crossed ... (*Holds her skirt down on her knees.*)

GUERRILLERA: Come with me and help make the revolution!

MARTYR 3: Let's go, kill'em, kill'em!

GUERRILLERA: Good things will come to pass. Come with me and rebel!

MARTYR 3: Let's go! (*To the others.*) Come on!

MARTYR 2: All right, let's go!
MARTYR 1: Bueno . . .
ALL: Let's go, vamos! ¡Sí! ¡Arriba! ¡Vamos! Come on come on!

MARTYR 3 *picks up a broom and rests it on her shoulder like a rifle. The others follow suit. All sing.*

SI ADELITA SE FUERA CON OTRO
LA SEGUIRÍA POR TIERRA Y POR MAR
SI POR MAR EN UN BUQUE DE GUERRA
SI POR TIERRA EN UN TREN MILITAR

GUERRILLERA: But first . . . hold it, hold it . . . but first . . . we must peel the potatoes, cook the rice, make the menudo and sweep the hall . . . (*The* WOMEN *groan and lose enthusiasm.*) . . . because there's gonna be a fund raiser tonight!

Music begins. The GUERRILLERA *and* WOMEN *sing.*

GUERRILLERA:
THERE'S GONNA BE A FUND-RAISER
THE BROTHERS WILL SPEAK OF CHANGE

CHORUS:
WE GONNA HAVE BANANA SURPRISE
WE GONNA CUT YAUTÍAS IN SLICE
THERE'S GONNA BE A FUND-RAISER
BUT THEY'LL ASK US TO PEEL AND FRY

GUERRILLERA:
WE SAY OKAY
WE WILL FIGHT NOT CLEAN
BUT THEY SAY GO DEAR
AND TYPE THE SPEECH

ANITA IS GONNA MAKE IT
SHE'S GONNA MAKE IT

CHORUS:
MARÍA WILL SWEEP THE FLOOR
JUANITA IS FAT AND PREGNANT
PREGNANT FOR WHAT
NO MATTER IF WE'RE TIRED
AS LONG LONG LONG LONG
AS LONG AS THEY'RE NOT

TONIGHT TONIGHT
TONIGHT TONIGHT
TONIGHT TONIGHT
TONIGHT TONIGHT

GUERRILLERA:
WON'T BE JUST ANY NIGHT

CHORUS:
TONIGHT TONIGHT
TONIGHT TONIGHT
TONIGHT TONIGHT
TONIGHT TONIGHT

GUERRILLERA:
WE'LL BE NO MORE HARRASSED

CHORUS:
TONIGHT TONIGHT
TONIGHT TONIGHT
TONIGHT TONIGHT
TONIGHT TONIGHT

GUERRILLERA:
I'LL HAVE SOMETHING TO SAY

CHORUS:
TONIGHT TONIGHT

GUERRILLERA:
FOR US A NEW DAY WILL START

CHORUS:
TODAY THE WOMEN
WANT THE HOURS

GUERRILLERA:
HOURS TO BE LOVING

CHORUS:
TODAY THE WOMEN
WANT THE HOURS

GUERRILLERA:	CHORUS:
AND STILL THE TIME TO FIGHT	BORING BORING
TO MAKE THIS ENDLESS	BORING BORING
BORING BORING BORING	BORING BORING
BORING BORING BORING	BORING BORING
FLIGHT!	FLIGHT!

All end the song with mops and brooms upraised. A voice is heard offstage.

MAN: (*Offstage.*) Is dinner ready! (*The* WOMEN *drop their "weapons" and run away.*)

WOMAN 1: ¡Ay, se me quema el arroz!

WOMAN 2: ¡Bendito, las habichuelas!

WOMAN 3: ¡Ay, Virgen de Guadalupe, las enchiladas! (*They exit.*)

GUERRILLERA: (*Exiting after them.*) Wait! Wait! What about the revolution! ... (*Black out.*)

As the lights go up the MAN *enters dressed as a campesino, with poncho and sombrero. The* SOCIAL RESEARCHER *enters right behind. She holds a notebook and a pencil.*

RESEARCHER: (*With an accent.*) Excuse me señor ... buenas tardes. Me llamo Miss Smith. I'm from the Peaceful Corps. Could you be so kind to answer some questions for me—for our research study?

MAN: Bueno.

RESEARCHER: Have you many children?

MAN: God has not been good to me. Of sixteen children born, only nine live.

RESEARCHER: Does you wife work?

MAN: No. She stays at home.

RESEARCHER: I see. How does she spend the day?

MAN: (*Scratching his head.*) Well, she gets up at four in the morning, fetches water and wood, makes the fire and cooks breakfast. Then she goes to the river and washes the clothes. After that she goes to town to get the corn ground and buy what we need in the market. Then she cooks the midday meal.

RESEARCHER: You come home at midday?

MAN: No, no, she brings the meal to me in the field—about three kilometers from home.

RESEARCHER: And after that?

MAN: Well, she takes care of the hens and the pigs ... and of course, she looks after the children all day ... then she prepares supper so it is ready when I come home.

RESEARCHER: Does she go to bed after supper?

MAN: No, I do. She has things to do around the house until about ten o'clock.

RESEARCHER: But, señor, you said your wife doesn't work ...

MAN: Of course, she doesn't work. I told you, she stays home!

RESEARCHER: (*Closing notebook.*) Thank you, señor. You have been very helpful. Adiós. (*She exits. The* MAN *follows her.*)

MAN: Hey, psst, señorita ... my wife goes to bed at ten o'clock. I can answer more questions for you later ... (*Black out.*)

In the dark we hear the beginning of "Dolphins by the Beach." The DAUGHTER 1 *and the* GIRL *enter. They dance to the music. This dance portrays the fantasies of a young woman. It is a dance of freedom and self-realization. A Fanfare is heard, breaking the spell. They run away. The MC enters.*

MC: Ladies and gentlemen, señoras y señores ... the show goes on and on and on and ON! The beauty, the talent, the endurance of these contestants is, you have to agree, OVERWHELMING. They have gone beyond the call of duty in pursuit of their goal. They have performed unselfishly. They have given their all. And will give even more, for, ladies and gentlemen, señoras y señores, the contest is not over yet. As the excitement mounts—I can feel it in the air!—the question burning in everyone's mind is: who will be the winner? (*As soap opera narrator.*) Who will wear that crown on that pretty little head? What will she do? Will she laugh? Will she cry? Will she faint in my arms? ... Stay tuned for the last chapter of Reina for a Day! (*MC exits. All the women enter.*)

DAUGHTER 1: Mamá, may I go out and play? It is such a beautiful day and the tree is full of mangoes. May I get some? Let me go out to the top of the hill. Please. I just want to sit there and look ahead, far away. If I squint my eyes real hard I think I can see the ocean. Mami, please, may I, may I go out?

MOTHER: Niña, what nonsense. Your head is always in the clouds. I can't give you permission to go out. Wait until your father comes home and ask him. (*Father enters.*)

DAUGHTER 1: Papá, please, may I go out and play? It is such a beautiful day and ...

FATHER: No. Stay home with your mother. Girls belong at home. You are becoming much of a tomboy. Why don't you learn to cook, to sew, to mend my socks ...

WIFE: Husband, I would like to buy some flowers for the windows, and that vase I saw yesterday at the shop ...

HUSBAND: Flowers, flowers, vases. What luxury! Instead of such fuss about the house, why don't you do something about having a child? I want a son. We've been married two years now and I am tired of waiting. What's the matter with you? People are already talking. It's me they suspect ...

MOTHER: Son, I have placed all my hopes on you. I hope you will be better than your father and take care of me ...

SON: I'm going off to the war. I have been called to play the game of death. I must leave you now. I must go and kill ...

WIDOW: He gave his life for the country in a far away land, killing people he didn't know, people who didn't speak his language. I'm with child. His child. I hope it's a son ... he wanted a son so much ...

DAUGHTER 2: Mother, I'm pregnant. He doesn't want to get married. I don't want to get married. I don't even know whether I want this child ...

MOTHER: Hija ... how can you do this to me?! How is it possible. That's not what I taught you! I ... your father ... your brother ... the neighbors ... what would people say?

BROTHER: I'll kill him. I know who did it. I'll wring his neck. He'll pay for this! Abusador sin escrúpulos ... Dishonoring decent girls ... And I thought he was my friend. He'll pay dearly for my sister's virginity. ¡Lo pagará con sangre!

DAUGHTER 1: But I read it in *Cosmopolitan.* It said everyone is doing it! And the TV commercials ... and ...

MOTHER: Hijo, what's the matter? You look worried ...

SON: Mother, my girlfriend is having a baby. My baby. I want to bring her here. You know, I don't have a job, and well, her parent's kicked her out of the house ...

MOTHER: Just like his father! So young and already spilling his seed around like a generous spring shower. Bring her. Bring your woman to me. I hope she has wide hips and gives you many healthy sons. (MOTHER *and* SON *exit.*)

The WOMEN *make moaning sounds, moving around, grouping and regrouping. Loud Latin music bursts on. The* WOMEN *dance frenetically, then suddenly the music stops.*

WOMAN 1: Sometimes, while I dance, I hear—behind the rhythmically shuffling feet—the roar of the water cascading down the mountain, thrown against the cliffs by an enraged ocean.

WOMAN 2: ... I hear the sound of water in a shower, splattering against the tiles where a woman lies dead. I hear noises beyond the water, and sometimes they frighten me.

WOMAN 3: Behind the beat of the drums I hear the thud of a young woman's body thrown from a roof. I hear the screeching of wheels from a speeding car and the stifled cries of a young girl lying on the street.

WOMAN 4: Muffled by the brass section I sometimes hear in the distance desperate cries of help from elevators, parking lots and apartment buildings. I hear the echoes in a forest: "please ... no ... don't ... " of a child whimpering.

WOMAN 1: I think I hear my sister cry while we dance.

WOMAN 2: I hear screams. I hear the terrorized sounds of a young girl running naked along the highway.

WOMAN 3: The string section seems to murmur names ...

WOMAN 4: To remind me that the woman, the girl who at this very moment is being beaten ...

WOMAN 1: raped ...

WOMAN 2: murdered ...

WOMAN 3: is my sister ...

WOMAN 4: my daughter ...

WOMAN 1: my mother ...

ALL: myself ...

The WOMEN *remain on stage, backs turned to the audience.*

We hear a fanfare. The MC *enters.*

MC: Ladies and gentlemen, the choice has been made, the votes have been counted, the results are in ... and the winner is ... señoras y señores: the queen of queens, Miss Señorita Mañana! There she is ... (*Music from Miss America's "There She is ... ". The* GIRL *enters followed by Mamá. The* GIRL *is wearing all the items she has picked from previous scenes: the tinsel crown, the flowers, a mantilla, etc. Her face is still made up as a clown. The* WOMEN *turn around to look. The* GIRL *looks upset, restless with all the manipulation she has endured. The* WOMEN *are distressed by what they see. They surround the* GIRL.)

WOMAN 1: This is not what I meant at all ...

WOMAN 2: I meant ...

WOMEN 3: I don't know what I meant.

WOMAN 4: I think we goofed. She's a mess. (*They look at Mamá reproachfully. Mamá looks apologetic.*)

MAMA: I only wanted ...

WOMAN 1: (*Pointing to the* MC.) It's all his fault!

MC: Me? I only wanted to make her a queen! Can we go on with the contest? This is a waste of time ...

WOMAN 2: You and your fff ... contest!

WOMAN 3: Cálmate, chica. Wait.

WOMAN 4: (*To* MC.) Look, we have to discuss this by ourselves. Give us a break, Okay?

MC: (*Mumbling as he exits.*) What do they want? What's the matter with them? ...

WOMAN 1: (*To* GIRL.) Ven acá, m'ija. (*The* WOMEN *take off, one by one, all the various items, clean her face, etc.*)

WOMAN 2: Honey, this is not what it is about ...

WOMAN 3: I'm not sure yet what it's about ...

WOMAN 4: It is about what really makes you a woman.

WOMAN 1: It is not the clothes.

WOMAN 2: Or the hair.

WOMAN 3: Or the lipstick.

WOMAN 4: Or the cooking.

WOMAN 3: But ... what is it about?

WOMAN 4: Well ... I was 13 when the blood first arrived. My mother locked herself in the bathroom with me, and recited the facts of life, and right then and there, very solemnly, she declared me a woman.

WOMAN 1: I was 18 when, amid pain and pleasure, my virginity floated away in a sea of blood. He held me tight and said "now I have made you a woman."

WOMAN 2: Then, from my insides a child burst forth ... crying, bathed in blood and other personal substances. And then someone whispered in my ear: "Now you are a real real woman."

WOMAN 3: In their songs they have given me the body of a mermaid, of a palm tree, of an ample-hipped guitar. In the movies I see myself as a whore, a nymphomaniac, a dumb servant or a third-rate dancer. I look for myself and I can't find me. I only find someone else's idea of me.

MAMA: But think ... what a dangerous, deadly adventure being a woman! The harassment of being a woman ... So many parts to be played so many parts to be stiffled and denied. But look at so many wild, free young things crying, like the fox in the story: "tame me, tame and I'll be yours!"

WOMAN 1: But I'm tired of stories!

WOMAN 2: Yes, enough of "be this," "do that!"

WOMAN 3: "Look like that!" Mira, mira!

WOMAN 4: "Buy this product!"

WOMAN 1: "Lose 10 pounds!"

MAMA: Wait, wait some more, and maybe, just maybe ...

WOMAN 1: Tell my daughter that I love her ...

WOMAN 2: Tell my daughter I wish I had really taught her the facts of life ...

WOMAN 3: Tell my daughter that still there are mysteries ...

WOMAN 4: ... that the life I gave her doesn't have to be like mine.

THE GIRL: ... that there are possibilities. That women that go crazy in the night, that women that die alone and frustrated, that women that exist only in the mind, are only half of the story, because a woman is ...

WOMAN 1: A fountain of fire!

WOMAN 2: A river of love!

WOMAN 3: An ocean of strength!

WOMAN 4: Mirror, mirror on the wall ...

They look at each other as images on a mirror, discovering themselves in each other. The GIRL *is now one of them. She steps out and sings:*

"DON'T DENY US THE MUSIC"

WOMAN IS A FOUNTAIN OF FIRE
WOMAN IS A RIVER OF LOVE
A LATIN WOMAN IS JUST A WOMAN
WITH THE MUSIC INSIDE

DON'T DENY US THE MUSIC
DON'T IMAGINE MY FACE
I'VE FOUGHT MANY BATTLES
I'VE SUNG MANY SONGS
I AM JUST A WOMAN
WITH THE MUSIC INSIDE

I AM JUST A WOMAN BREAKING
THE LINKS OF A CHAIN
I AM JUST A WOMAN
WITH THE MUSIC INSIDE

FREE THE BUTTERFLY
LET THE OCEANS ROLL IN
FREE THE BUTTERFLY
LET THE OCEANS ROLL IN
I AM ONLY A WOMAN
WITH THE MUSIC INSIDE

Coser y cantar

A One-Act Bilingual Fantasy for Two Women
1981

Coser y Cantar

CHARACTERS

ELLA, una mujer
SHE, the same woman
The action takes place in an apartment in New York City in the present/past.

SET

A couch, a chair, and a dressing table with an imaginary mirror facing the audience is on each side of the stage. A low table with a telephone on it is upstage center. In the back, a low shelf or cabinet holds a recordplayer, records and books. There are back exits on stage right and stage left.

Stage right is ELLA's area. Stage left is SHE's. Piles of books, magazines and newspapers surround SHE's area. A pair of ice skates and a tennis racket are visible somewhere. Her dressing table has a glass with pens and pencils and various bottles of vitamin pills. SHE wears jogging shorts and sneakers.

ELLA's area is somewhat untidy. Copies of *Cosmopolitan, Vanidades* and *TV Guías* are seen around her bed. ELLA's table is crowded with cosmetics, a figurine of the Virgen de la Caridad and a candle. A large conch and a pair of maracas are visible. ELLA is dressed in a short red kimono.

IMPORTANT NOTE FROM THE AUTHOR

This piece is really one long monologue. The two women are one and are playing a verbal, emotional game of ping pong. Throughout the action, except in the final confrontation, ELLA and SHE never look at each other, acting independently, pretending the other one does not really exist, although each continuously trespasses on each other's thoughts, feelings and behavior.

This play must NEVER be performed in just one language.

Coser y Cantar was first performed at Duo Theater in New York City on June 25, 1981 with the following cast:

ELLA .... Elizabeth Peña
SHE .... María Normán

It was directed by María Norman. The play has had many subsequent productions throughout the U.S. and in Puerto Rico. It was first published in *Tramoya*, the theater magazine of Universidad Veracruzana and Rutgers University, Issue No. 22, Jan.–Mar. 1990.

ACT I

In the dark we hear "Qué sabes tú", a recording by Olga Guillot. As lights go up slowly on ELLA'*s couch we see a naked leg up in the air, then a hand slides up the leg and begins to apply cream to it.* ELLA *puts cream on both legs, sensually, while singing along with the record.* ELLA *sits up in bed, takes a hairbrush, brushes her hair, then using the brush as a microphone continues to sing along. Carried away by the song,* ELLA *gets out of bed and "performs" in front of the imaginary mirror by her dressing table. At some point during the previous scene, lights will go up slowly on the other couch.* SHE *is reading* Psychology Today *magazine. We don't see her face at the beginning. As* ELLA *is doing her act by the mirror,* SHE'*s eyes are seen above the magazine. She stares ahead for a while. Then shows impatience.* SHE *gets up and turns off the recordplayer, cutting off* ELLA'*s singing in mid-sentence.* SHE *begins to pick up newspapers and magazines from the floor and to stack them up neatly.*

ELLA: (*With contained exasperation.*) ¿Por qué haces eso? ¡Sabes que no me gusta que hagas eso! Detesto que me interrumpas así. ¡Yo no te interrumpo cuando tú te imaginas que eres Barbra Streisand!

SHE: (*To herself, looking for her watch.*) What time is it? (*Finds watch.*) My God, twelve thirty! The day half-gone and I haven't done a thing .... And so much to be done. So much to be done. (*Looks at one of the newspapers she has picked up.*) ... Three people have been shot already. For no reason at all. No one is safe out there. No one. Not even those who speak good English. Not even those who know who they are ...

ELLA: (*Licking her lips.*) Revoltillo de huevos, tostadas, queso blanco, café con leche. Hmmm, eso es lo que me pide el estómago. Anoche soñé con ese desayuno.

ELLA *goes backstage singing "Es mi vivir una linda guajirita". We hear the sound of pots and pans over her singing. At the same time,* SHE *puts on the Jane Fonda exercise record and begins to do exercises in the middle of the room. Still singing,* ELLA *returns with a tray loaded with breakfast food and turns off the record player.* ELLA *sits on the floor, Japanese-style, and begins to eat.* SHE *sits also and takes a glass of orange juice.*

SHE: Do you have to eat so much? You eat all day, then lie there like a dead octopus.

ELLA: Y tú me lo recuerdas todo el día, pero si no fuera por todo lo que yo como, ya tú te hubieras muerto de hambre. (ELLA *eats.* SHE *sips her orange juice.*)

SHE: (*Distracted.*) What shall I do today? There's so much to do.

ELLA: (*With her mouth full.*) Sí, mucho. El problema siempre es, por dónde empezar.

SHE: I should go out and jog a couple of miles.

ELLA: (*Taking a bite of food.*) Sí. Debía salir a correr. Es bueno para la figura. (*Takes another bite.*) Y el corazón. (*Takes another bite.*) Y la circulación. (*Another bite.*) A correr se ha dicho. (ELLA *continues eating.* SHE *gets up and opens an imaginary window facing the audience.* SHE *looks out, breathes deeply, stretches.*)

SHE: Aaah, what a beautiful day! It makes you so ... so happy to be alive!

ELLA: (*From the table, without much enthusiasm.*) No es para tanto.

SHE: (SHE *goes to her dressing table, sits down takes pen and paper.*) I'll make a list of all the things I must do. Let's see. I should start from the inside .... Number one, clean the house ...

ELLA: (*Still eating*) Uno, limpiar la casa.

SHE: Two, take the garbage out.

ELLA: Dos, sacar la basura.

SHE: Then, do outside things. After running, I have to do something about El Salvador.

ELLA: Salvar a El Salvador.

SHE: Go to the march at the U.N.

ELLA: (*Has finished eating, picks up tray, gets enthusiasitc about the planning.*) Escribir una carta el editor del *New York Times.*

SHE: Aha, that too. (*Adds it to the list.*) How about peace in the Middle East?

ELLA: La cuestión del aborto.

SHE: Should that come after or before the budget cuts?

ELLA: (*With relish*) Comprar chorizos mexicanos para unos burritos.

SHE: (*Writing.*) See that new Fassbinder film. (ELLA *makes a "boring" face.*) Find the map ... (SHE *writes.*)

ELLA: (*Serious.*) Ver a mi madrina. Tengo algo que preguntarle a los caracoles. (*Splashes Florida Water around her head.*)

SHE: (*Exasperated.*) Not again! ... (*Thinks.*) Buy a fish tank. (*Writes it down.*)

ELLA: ¿Una pecera?

SHE: I want to buy a fish tank, and some fish. I read in *Psychology Today* that it is supposed to calm your nerves to watch fish swimming in a tank.

ELLA: (*Background music begins.*) Peceras. (*Sits at her dressing table. Stares into the mirror. Gets lost in memories.*) Las peceras me recuerdan el aeropuerto cuando me fui ... los que se iban, dentro de la pecera. Esperando. Esperando dentro de aquel cuarto transparente. Al otro lado del cristal, los otros, los que se quedaban: los padres, los hermanos, los tíos .... Allí estábamos, en la pecera, nadando en el mar que nos salía por los ojos ... Y los que estaban dentro y los que estaban afuera solo podían mirarse. Mirarse las caras distorcionadas por las lágrimas y el cristal sucio—lleno de huellas de manos que se querían tocar, empañado por el aliento de bocas que trataban de besarse a través del cristal .... Una pecera llena de peces asustados, que no sabían nadar, que no sabían de las aguas heladas ... donde los tiburones andan con pistolas ...

SHE: (*Scratches item off the list forcefully.*) Dwelling in the past takes energies away.

ELLA: (ELLA *looks for the map among objects on her table. Lifts the Virgen de la Caridad statue.*) ¿Dónde habré puesto el mapa? Juraría que estaba debajo de la Santa ... (ELLA *looks under the bed. Finds one old and dirty tennis shoe. It seems to bring back memories.*) Lo primerito que yo pensaba hacer al llegar aquí era comprarme unos tenis bien cómodos y caminar todo Nueva York. Cuadra por cuadra. Para saber dónde estaba todo.

SHE: I got the tennis shoes—actually, they were basketball shoes ... But I didn't get to walk every block as I had planned. I wans't aware of how big the city was. I wasn't aware of muggers either ... I did get to walk a lot, though ... in marches and demonstrations. But by then, I had given up wearing tennis shoes. I was into boots ....

ELLA: ... Pero nunca me perdí en el subway ...

SHE: Somehow I always knew where I was going. Sometimes the place I got to was the wrong place, to be sure. But that's different. All I had to do was choose another place ... and go to it. I have gotten to a lot of right places too.

ELLA: (*With satisfaction.*) Da gusto llegar al lugar que se va sin perder el camino.

Loud gunshots are heard outside, then police sirens, loud noises, screams, screeches. Both women get very nervous and upset. They run to the window and back, not knowing what to do.

SHE: There they go again! Now they are shooting the birds on the trees!

ELLA: ¡Están matando las viejitas en el parque …

SHE: Oh, my God! Let's get out of here!

ELLA: … Y los perros que orinan en los hidrantes!

SHE: No, no. Let's stay here! Look! They've shot a woman riding a bicycle … and now somebody is stealing it!

ELLA: ¡La gente corre, pero nadie hace nada!

SHE: Are we safe? Yes, we are safe. We're safe here … No, we're not! They can shoot through the window!

ELLA: ¡La gente grita pero nadie hace nada!

SHE: Get away from the window!

ELLA: (*Pausa.*) Pero, ¿y todo lo que hay que hacer?

They look around undecided, then begin to do several things around the room, but then drop them immediately. SHE *picks up a book.* ELLA *goes to the kitchen. We hear the rattling of pots and pans.* ELLA *returns eating leftovers straight from a large pot.* ELLA *sits in front of the mirror, catches sight of herself. Puts pot down, touches her face, tries different smiles, none of which is a happy smile.* SHE *is lying on the couch staring at the ceiling.*

ELLA: Si pudiera sonreír como la Mona Lisa me tomarían por misteriosa en vez de antipática porque no enseño los dientes …

SHE: (*From the couch, still staring at the ceiling.*) That's because your face is an open book. You wear your emotions all over, like a suntan … You are emotionally naive … or rather, emotionally primitive … perhaps even emotionally retarded. What you need is a … a certain emotional sophistication …

ELLA: … sí, claro, eso … sofisticación emocional … (*Thinks about it*) … sofisticación emocional … ¿Y qué carajo es sofisticación emocional? ¿Ser como tú? ¡Tú, que ya ni te acuerdas como huele tu propio sudor, que no reconoces el sonido de tu propia voz! ¡No me jodas!

SHE: See what I mean! (SHE *gets up, goes to her dressing table, looks for the map.*)

ELLA: (*Exasperated.*) ¡Ay, Dios mío, ¿qué habré hecho yo para merecérmela? Es como tener un … un pingüino colgado del cuello!

SHE: An albatross ... you mean like an albatross around your neck. Okay, Okay ... I'll make myself light, light as a feather ... light as an albatross feather. I promise. (SHE *continues to look for the map.*) Where did I put that map? I thought it was with the passport, the postcards ... the traveling mementos ... (*continues looking among papers kept in a small box. Finds her worry beads. That brings memories. She plays with the beads for a while.*) ... I never really learned how to use them ... (ELLA *continues searching elsewhere.*) Do you know what regret means?

ELLA: (*Absentmindedly.*) Es una canción de Edith Piaff.

SHE: Regret means that time in Athens, many years ago ... at a cafe where they played bouzuki music. The men got up and danced and broke glasses and small dishes against the tiled floor. The women did not get up to dance. They just watched and tapped their feet under the table ... now and then shaking their shoulders to the music. One Greek man danced more than the others. He broke more glasses and dishes than the others. His name was Nikos. It was his birthday. He cut his hand with one of the broken glasses. But he didn't stop, he didn't pay any attention to his wound. He kept on dancing. He danced by my table. I took a gardenia from the vase on the table and gave it to him. He took it, rubbed it on the blood dripping from his hand and gave it back to me with a smile. He danced away to other tables ... . I wanted to get up and break some dishes and dance with him. Dance away, out the door, into the street, all the way to some cheap hotel by the harbor, where next morning I would hang the bedsheet stained with my blood out the window. But I didn't get up. Like the Greek women, I stayed on my seat, tapping my feet under the table, now and then shaking my shoulders to the music ... a bloodied gardenia wilting in my glass of retsina ...

ELLA: No haber roto ni un plato. That's regret for sure.

The clock strikes the hour. Alarmed, they get up quickly and look for their shoes.

SHE: (*Putting boots on. Rushed, alarmed.*) I have to practice the speech!

ELLA: (*Puts on high heels.*) Sí, tienes que aprender a hablar más alto. Sin micrófono no se te oye. Y nunca se sabe si habrá micrófono. Es mejor depender de los pulmones que de los aparatos. Los aparatos a veces fallan en el momento más inoportuno.

They stand back to back, each facing stage left and stage right respectively. They speak at the same time.

SHE: (*In English.*) A E I O U,
ELLA: (*In Spanish.*) A E I O U .
ELLA: Pirámides.
SHE: Pyramids.
ELLA: Orquídeas.
SHE: Orchids.
ELLA: Sudor.
SHE: Sweat.
ELLA: Luz.
SHE: Light.
ELLA: Blood.
SHE: Sangre.
ELLA: Dolphins.
SHE: Delfines.
ELLA: Mountains.
SHE: Montañas.
ELLA: Sed.
SHE: Thirst.

Freeze. Two beats. They snap out of their concentration.

ELLA: Tengo sed.
SHE: I think I'll have a Diet Pepsi.
ELLA: Yo me tomaría un guarapo de caña. (SHE *goes to the kitchen.*)
ELLA: (*Looking for the map. Stops before the mirror and looks at her body, passes hand by hips, sings a few lines of "Macorina" and continues to look for the map behind furniture, along the walls, etc. Suddenly, it seems as if* ELLA *hears something from the apartment next door.* ELLA *puts her ear to the wall and listens more carefully. Her face shows confusion.* ELLA *asks herself, deeply, seriously intrigued.*) ¿Por qué sería que Songo le dió a Borondongo? ¿Sería porque Borondongo le dió a Bernabé? ¿O porque Bernabé le pegó a Muchilanga? ¿O en realidad sería porque Muchilanga le echó burundanga? (*Pause.*) ... ¿Y Monina? ¿Quién es Monina? ¡Ay, nunca lo he entendido ... el gran misterio de nuestra cultura! (SHE *returns drinking a Diet Pepsi. Sits on the bed and drinks*

slowly, watching the telephone with intense concentration. ELLA'*s attention is also drawn to the telephone. Both watch it hypnotically.*) El teléfono no ha sonado hoy.

SHE: I must call mother. She's always complaining.

ELLA: Llamadas. Llamadas. ¿Por qué no llamará? Voy a concentrarme para que llame. (*Concentrates.*) El teléfono sonará en cualquier momento. Ya. Ya viene. Suena. Sí. Suena. Va a sonar.

SHE: (*Sitting in the lotus position, meditating.*) Ayer is not the same as yesterday.

ELLA: Estás loca.

SHE: I think I'm going crazy. Talking to myself all day.

ELLA: It must be. It's too soon for menopause.

SHE: Maybe what I need is a good fuck after all.

ELLA: Eres una enferma.

SHE: At least let's talk about something important—exercise our intellects.

ELLA: ¿Como qué?

SHE: We could talk about ... about ... the meaning of life.

ELLA: Mi mamá me dijo una vez que la vida, sobre todo la vida de una mujer, era coser y cantar. Y yo me lo creí. Pero ahora me doy cuenta que la vida, la de todo el mundo: hombre, mujer, perro, gato, jicotea, es, en realidad, comer y cagar ... ¡en otras palabras, la misma mierda!

SHE: Puke! So much for philosophy.

Both look among the books and magazines. ELLA *picks up* Vanidades *magazine, flips through the pages.* SHE *starts reading* Self *magazine.*

ELLA: No sé que le ha pasado a *Corín Tellado.* Ya sus novelas no son tan románticas como antes. Me gustaban más cuando ella, la del sedoso cabello castaño y los brazos torneados y los ojos color violeta, no se entregaba así, tan fácilmente, a él, el hombre, que aunque más viejo, y a veces cojo, pero siempre millonario, la deseaba con locura, pero la respetaba hasta el día de la boda ...

SHE: I can't believe you're reading that crap.

ELLA: (*Flipping through the pages some more.*) Mira, esto es interesante: ¡un test! "Usted y sus Fantasías". A ver, lo voy hacer. (*Gets a pencil from the table.*) Pregunta número uno: ¿Tienes fantasías a menudo? (*Piensa.*)

SHE: Yes. (ELLA *writes down answer.*)

ELLA: ¿Cuán a menudo? (*Thinks.*)

SHE: Every night ... and day.

ELLA: (*Writes down answer.*) ¿Cuál es el tema recurrente de tus fantasías?

SHE: (*Sensually mischievous.*) I am lying naked. Totally, fully, wonderfully naked. Feeling good and relaxed. Suddenly, I feel something warm and moist between my toes. It is a tongue! A huge, wide, live tongue! The most extraordinary thing about this tongue is that it changes. It takes different shapes ... It wraps itself around my big toe ... then goes in between and around each toe ... then it moves up my leg, up my thigh ... and into my ...

ELLA: ¡Vulgar! No se trata de esas fantasías. Se trata de ... de ... de ¡Juana de Arco!

SHE: I didn't know that Joan of Arc was into ...

ELLA: Ay, chica, no hablaba de fantasías eróticas, sino de fantasías *heróicas* ... a lo Juana de Arco. A mí Juana de Arco me parece tan dramática, tan patriótica, tan sacrificada ...

SHE: I don't care for Joan of Arc—too hot to handle! ... ha, ha, ha. (*Both laugh at the bad joke.*)

ELLA: (*Picking up the chair and lifting it above her head.*) Mi fantasía es ser una superwoman: ¡Maravilla, la mujer maravilla! (*Puts chair down and lies across it, arms and legs kicking in the air, as if swimming.*) ... Y salvar a una niña que se ahoga en el Canal de la Mancha, y nadar, como Esther Williams, hasta los blancos farallones de Dover ... (*Gets up, then rides astride the chair.*) ¡Ser una heroína que cabalgando siempre adelante, hacia el sol, inspirada por una fe ciega, una pasión visionaria, arrastre a las multitudes para juntos salvar al mundo de sus errores!

SHE: Or else, a rock singer! They move crowds, all right. And make more money. How about, La Pasionaria and her Passionate Punk Rockers!

ELLA: (*Disappointed.*) Tú nunca me tomas en serio.

SHE: My fantasy is to make people happy. Make them laugh. I'd rather be a clown. When times are as bad as these, it is better to keep the gathering gloom at bay by laughing and dancing. The Greeks do it, you know. They dance when they are sad. Yes, what I really would like to be is a dancer. And dance depression ... inflation ... and the NUCLEAR THREAT ... AWAY!

ELLA: (*To herself, disheartened.*) Pero tienes las piernas muy flacas y el culo muy grande.

SHE: (*Ignoring* ELLA*'s remarks.*) Dancing is what life is all about.

The tap- tapping of a hundred feet on Forty-Second Street is more exciting than an army marching off to kill the enemy . . . . Yes! My fantasy is to be a great dancer . . . like Fred Astaire and Ginger Rogers!

ELLA: ¿Cuál de ellos, Fred Astaire o Ginger Rogers?

SHE: Why can't I be both?

ELLA: ¿Será que eres bisexual?

SHE: (*Puts her head betwen her legs, as if exercising.*) No. I checked out. Just one.

ELLA: ¿Nunca has querido ser hombre?

SHE: Not really. Men are such jerks.

ELLA: Pero se divierten más. ¿De veras que nunca te has sentido como ese poema?: " . . . Hoy, quiero ser hombre. Subir por las tapias, burlar los conventos, ser todo un Don Juan; raptar a Sor Carmen y a Sor Josefina, rendirlas, y a Julia de Burgos violar . . . "

SHE: You are too romantic, that's your problem.

ELLA: ¡Y tú eres muy promiscua! Te acuestas con demasiada gente que ni siquiera te cae bien, que no tiene nada que ver contigo.

SHE: (*Flexing her muscles.*) It keeps me in shape. (*Bitchy.*) And besides, it isn't as corny as masturbating, listening to boleros.

ELLA: (*Covering her ears.*) ¡Cállate! ¡Cállate! ¡Cállate! (*Goes to the window and looks out.) (Pause.*) Está nevando. No se ve nada allá afuera. Y aquí, estas cuatro paredes me están volviendo . . . ¡bananas! (ELLA *goes to the table, takes a banana and begins to eat it.* SHE *plays with an old tennis racket.*) Si por lo menos tuviera el televisor, podría ver una película o algo . . . pero, no . . .

SHE: Forget about the TV set.

ELLA: ¡Tuviste que tirarlo por la ventana! Y lo peor no es que me quedé sin televisor. No. Lo peor es el caso por daños y perjuicios que tengo pendiente.

SHE: I don't regret a thing.

ELLA: La mala suerte que el maldito televisor le cayera encima al carro de los Moonies que viven al lado. ¿Te das cuenta? ¡Yo, acusada de terrorista por el Reverendo Sun Myung Moon! ¡A nadie le pasa esto! ¡A nadie más que a mí! ¡Te digo que estoy cagada de aura tiñosa!

SHE: You are exagerating. Calm down.

ELLA: Cada vez que me acuerdo me hierve la sangre. Yo, yo, ¡acusada de terrorista! ¡Yo! ¡Cuando la víctima he sido yo!

¡No se puede negar que yo soy una víctima del terrorismo!

SHE: Dont' start with your paranoia again.

ELLA: ¡Paranoia! ¿Tú llamas paranoia a todo lo que ha pasado? ¿A lo que pasó con los gatos? ¡Mis tres gatos, secuestrados, descuartizados, y luego dejados en la puerta, envueltos en papel de regalo, con una tarjeta de Navidad!

SHE: You know very well it didn't happen like that.

ELLA: ¿Y la cobra entre las cartas? How about that snake in the mail box? Who put it there? Who? Who? Why?

SHE: Forget all that. Mira como te pones por gusto ... Shit! We should have never come here.

ELLA: (*Calming down.*) Bueno, es mejor que New Jersey. Además ¿cuál es la diferencia? El mismo tiroteo, el mismo cucaracheo, la misma mierda ... coser y cantar, you know.

SHE: At least in Miami there was sunshine ...

ELLA: Había sol, sí, pero demasiadas nubes negras. Era el humo que salía de tantos cerebros tratando de pensar. Además, aquí hay más cosas que hacer.

SHE: Yes. Más cosas que hacer. And I must do them. I have to stop contemplating my navel and wallowing in all this ... this ... Yes, one day soon I have to get my caca together and get out THERE and DO something. Definitely. Seriously. (*Silent pause. Both are lost in thought.*)

ELLA: I remember when I first met you ... there was a shimmer in your eyes ...

SHE: Y tú tenías una sonrisa ...

ELLA: And with that shimmering look in your eyes and that smile ...

SHE: ... pensamos que íbamos a conquistar el mundo ...

ELLA: ... But ...

SHE: ... I don't know ... (SHE *goes to her table and picks up a bottle of vitamins.*) Did I take my pills today?

ELLA: Sí.

SHE: Vitamin C?

ELLA: Sí.

SHE: Iron?

ELLA: Sí.

SHE: Painkiller?

ELLA: Of course ... because camarón que se duerme se lo lleva la corriente.

SHE: A shrimp that falls asleep is carried away by the current?

ELLA: No ... that doesn't make any sense.

SHE: Between the devil and the deep blue sea?

ELLA: ... No es lo mismo que entre la espada y la pared, porque del dicho al hecho hay un gran trecho.

SHE: Betwixt the cup and the lip you should not look a gift horse in the mouth.

ELLA: A caballo regalado no se le mira el colmillo, pero tanto va el cántaro a la fuente, hasta que se rompe.

SHE: An eye for an eye and a tooth for a tooth.

ELLA: Y no hay peor ciego que el que no quiere ver. (*Both are lethargic, about to fall asleep.*)

SHE: (*Yawning.*) I have to be more competitive.

ELLA: (*Yawning.*) Despues de la siesta.

They fall asleep. Lights dim out. In the background, music box music comes on and remains through ELLA*'s entire monologue.*

ELLA: (*Upset voice of a young child.*) Pero, ¿por qué tengo que esperar tres horas para bañarme? ¡No me va a pasar nada! ... ¡Los peces comen y hacen la digestión en el agua y no les pasa nada! ... Sí, tengo muchas leyes. ¡Debía ser abogada! ¡Debía ser piloto! ¡Debía ser capitán! ¡Debía ser una tonina y nadar al otro lado de la red, sin temer a los tiburones! (*Pause. Now as a rebelious teenager.*) ¡Y no voy a caminar bajo el sol con ese paraguas! ¡No me importa que la piel blanca sea mas elegante! ... ¡No se puede tapar el sol con una sombrilla! ¡No se puede esperar que la marea baje cuando tiene que subir! (*As an adult.*) ... No se puede ser un delfín en las pirámides. No se le puede cortar la cabeza al delfín y guardarla en la gaveta, entre las prendas más íntimas y olvidar el delfín. Y olvidar que se quiso ser el delfín. Olvidar que se quiso ser la niña desnuda, cabalgando sobre el delfín ...

SHE: (*Lights up on* SHE. *Needling.*) So, you don't have dreams. So, you can't remember your dreams. So, you never talk about your dreams. I think you *don't want* to remember your dreams. You always want to be going somewhere, but now you are stuck here with me, because outside it's raining blood and you have been to all the places you can possibly ever go to! No, you have nowhere to go! Nowhere! Nowhere! (ELLA *slaps* SHE *with force. The clock strikes twice. They awaken. Lights come up fully.* SHE *slaps herself softly on both cheeks.*) A nightmare in the middle of the day!

ELLA: Tengo que encontrar ese mapa. (*They look for the map.*)

SHE: (*Picks up a book, fans the pages. Finds a marker in one page.*

Reads silently, then reads aloud.) "Picasso's gaze was so absorbing one was surprised to find anything left on the paper after he looked at it . . . " (*Thinks about this image. Then softly.*) Think about that . . .

ELLA: Sí. Claro. Así siento mis ojos en la primavera. Después de ver tanto árbol desnudo durante el invierno, cuando salen las primeras hojas, esas hojitas de un verde tan tierno, me da miedo mirarlas mucho porque temo que mis ojos le vayan a chupar todo el color.

SHE: I miss all that green. Sometimes I wish I could do like Dorothy in "The Wizard of Oz" close my eyes, click my heels and repeat three times, "there's no place like home" . . . and, puff! be there.

ELLA: El peligro de eso es que una pueda terminar en una finca en Kansas.

SHE: . . . I remember that trip back home . . . I'd never seen such a blue sea. It was an alive, happy blue. You know what I mean?

ELLA: A mí no se me había olvidado. Es el mar más azul, el más verde . . . el más chévere del mundo. No hay comparación con estos mares de por aquí.

SHE: . . . It sort of slapped you in the eyes, got into them and massaged your eyeballs . . .

ELLA: Es un mar tan sexy, tan tibio. Como que te abraza. Dan ganas de quitarse el traje de baño y nadar desnuda . . . lo cual, por supuesto, hiciste a la primera oportunidad . . .

SHE: . . . I wanted to see everything, do everything in a week . . .

ELLA: (*Laughing.*) . . . No sé si lo viste todo, pero en cuanto a hacer . . . ¡el trópico te alborotó, chiquitica! ¡Hasta en el Malecón! ¡Qué escándalo!

SHE: (*Laughing.*) I sure let my hair down! It must have been all that rum. Everywhere we went, there was rum and "La Guantanamera" . . . And that feeling of belonging, of being home despite . . .

ELLA: (*Nostalgic.*) ¡Aaay!

SHE: ¿Qué pasa?

ELLA: ¡Ay, siento que me viene un ataque de nostalgia!

SHE: Let's wallow!

ELLA: ¡Ay, sí, un disquito!

SHE *puts a record on. It is "Nostalgia habanera" sung by Olga Guillot. Both sing and dance along with the record for a while. The music stays on throughout the scene.*

BOTH: (*Singing.*)

"Siento la nostalgia de volver a ti
más el destino manda y no puede ser
Mi Habana, mi tierra querida
cuándo yo te volveré a ver
Habana, como extraño el sol indiano de tus calles
Habana etc . . . ."

ELLA: ¡Aaay, esta nostalgia me ha dado un hambre!
SHE: That's the problem with nostalgia—it is usually loaded with calories! How about some steamed broccoli . . .
ELLA: Arroz . . .
SHE: Yogurt . . .
ELLA: Frijoles negros . . .
SHE: Bean sprouts . . .
ELLA: Plátanos fritos . . .
SHE: Wheat germ . . .
ELLA: Ensalada de aguacate . . .
SHE: Raw carrots . . .
ELLA: ¡Flan!
SHE: Granola!
ELLA: ¿Qué tal un arroz con pollo, o un ajiaco?
SHE: Let's go!

They exit out to the kitchen. Lights out. Record plays to the end. We hear rattling of pots and pans. When lights go up again, they lie on their respective beds.

ELLA: ¡Qué bien! ¡Qué rico! Esa comida me ha puesto erótica. I feel sexy. Romántica.
SHE: (*With bloated feeling.*) How can you feel sexy after rice and beans? . . . I feel violent, wild. I feel like . . . chains, leather, whips. Whish! Whish!
ELLA: No, no, no! Yo me siento como rosas y besos bajo la luna, recostada a una palmera mecida por el viento . . .
SHE: Such tropical, romantic tackiness, ay, ay, ay.
ELLA: Sí, . . . y un olor a jasmines que se cuela por la ventana . . .
SHE: I thought you were leaning on a swaying coconut tree.
ELLA: . . . Olor a jasmines, mezclado con brisas de salitre. A lo lejos se escucha un bolero: (*Sings.*)

"Te acuerdas de la noche de la playa
Te acuerdas que te di mi amor primero . . . "

SHE: ... I feel the smell of two bodies together, the heat of the flesh so close to mine, the sweat and the saliva trickling down my spine ... (*Both get progressively excited.*)

ELLA: ... y unas manos expertas me abren la blusa, me sueltan el ajustador, y con mucho cuidado, como si fueran dos mangos maduros, me sacan los senos al aire ...

SHE: ... And ten fingernails dig into my flesh and I hear drums beating faster and faster and faster!

They stop, exhaling a deep sigh of contentment. They get up from bed at different speeds and go to their dressing tables. ELLA *lights up a cigarette sensually.* SHE *puts cold cream on her face, slowly and sensually. They sing in a sexy, relaxed manner.*

ELLA: "Fumar es un placer ...

SHE: ... Genial, sensual ...

ELLA: ... Fumando espero ...

SHE: ... Al hombre que yo quiero ...

ELLA: ... Tras los cristales ...

SHE: ... De alegres ventanales ...

ELLA: ... Y mientras fumo ... "

SHE: (*Half laughs.*) ... I remember the first time ...

ELLA: Ja ja ... a mí me preguntaron si yo había tenido un orgasmo alguna vez. Yo dije que no. No porque no lo había tenido, sino porque no sabía lo que era ... Pensé que orgasmo era una tela.

SHE: I looked it up in the dictionary: orgasm. Read the definition, and still didn't know what it meant.

ELLA: A pesar del diccionario, hasta que no tuve el primero, en realidad no supe lo que quería decir ...

SHE: It felt wonderful. But all the new feelings scared me ...

ELLA: (*Kneeling on the chair.*) ... Fuí a la iglesia al otro día ... me arrodillé, me persigné, alcé los ojos al cielo —es decir al techo— muy devotamente, pero cuando empecé a pensar la oración ... me di cuenta de que, en vez de pedir perdón, estaba pidiendo ... aprobación! ... permiso para hacerlo otra vez!

SHE: ... Oh God, please, give me a sign! Tell me it is all right! Send an angel, una paloma, a flash of green light to give me the go ahead! Stamp upon me the Good Housekeeping Seal of Approval, to let me know that fucking is okay!

ELLA: ¡Ay, Virgen del Cobre! Yo tenía un miedo que se enterara la familia. ¡Me parecía que me lo leían en la cara!

They fall back laughing. The telephone rings three times. They stop laughing abruptly, look at the telephone with fear and expectation. After each ring each one in turn extends the hand to pick it up, but stops midway. Finally, after the third ring, SHE *picks it up.*

SHE: Hello? ... Oh, hiii, how are you? ... I am glad you called ... I wanted to ... Yes. Okay. Well, go ahead ... (*Listens.*) Yes, I know ... but I didn't think it was serious. (*Listens.*) ... You said our relationship was special, untouchable ... (*Whimpering.*) then how can you end it just like this ... I can't believe that all the things we shared don't mean anything to you anymore ... (*Listens.*) What do you mean, it was meaningful while it lasted?! ... Yes, I remember you warned me you didn't want to get involved ... but, all I said was that I love you ... Okay. I shouldn't have said that ... Oh, please, let's try again! ... Look ... I'll ... I'll come over Saturday night ... Sunday morning we'll make love ... have brunch: eggs, croissants, Bloody Marys ... we'll read the *Times* in bed and ... please, don't ... how can you? ...

ELLA: (*Having been quietly reacting to the conversation, and getting angrier and angrier* ELLA *grabs the phone away from* SHE.) ¿Pero quién carajo tú te crees que eres para venir a tirarme así, como si yo fuera una chancleta vieja? ¡Qué huevos fritos ni ocho cuartos, viejo! ¡Después de tanta hambre que te maté, los buenos vinos que te compré! ¡A ver si esa putica que te has conseguido cocina tan bien como yo! ¡A ver si esa peluá te va a dar todo lo que yo te daba! ¡A ver si esa guaricandilla ... (*Suddenly desperate.*) Ay, ¿cómo puedes hacerme esto a mí? ¡A mí que te adoro ciegamente, a mí, que te quiero tanto, que me muero por ti! ... Mi amor ... ay, mi amor, no me dejes. Haré lo que tú quieras. ¡Miénteme, pégame, traiciónme, patéame, arrástrame por el fango, pero no me dejes! (*Sobs. Listens. Calms down. Now stoically melodramatic and resigned.*) Está bien. Me clavas un puñal. Me dejas con un puñal clavado en el centro del corazón. Ya nunca podré volver a amar. Mi corazón se desangra, siento que me desvanezco ... Me iré a una playa solitaria y triste, y a media noche, como Alfonsina, echaré a andar hacia las olas y ... (*Listens for three beats. Gets angry.*) ¿Así es como respondes cuando vuelco mi corazón, mis sentimientos en tu oído? ¿Cuando mis lágrimas casi crean un corto circuito en el teléfono?! ¡Ay, infeliz! ¡Tú no sabes nada de la vida! Adiós, y que te vaya bien. De veras ... honestamente, no te guardo rencor ... te deseo lo mejor ... ¿Yo? ... yo seguiré mi viaje. Seré bien recibida en otros puertos. Ja, ja, ja ... De veras, te deseo de todo corazón que esa tipa, por lo menos, ¡sea tan BUENA EN LA CAMA COMO YO! (*Bangs the phone down. Both sit on the floor back to back. Long pause.* ELLA *fumes.* SHE *is contrite.*)

SHE: You shouldn't have said all those things.

ELLA: ¿Por qué no? Todo no se puede intelectualizar. You can't dance everything away, you know.

SHE: You can't eat yourself to numbness either.

ELLA: Yeah.

SHE: You know what's wrong with me? I can't relate any more. I have been moving away from people. I stay here and look at the ceiling. And talk to you. I don't know how to talk to people anymore. I don't know if I want to talk to people anymore!

ELLA: Tu problema es que ves demasiadas películas de Woody Allen, y ya te crees una neoyorquina neurótica. Yo no. Yo sé como tener una fiesta conmigo misma. Yo me divierto sola. Y me acompaño y me entretengo. Yo tengo mis recuerdos. Y mis plantas en la ventana. Yo tengo una solidez. Tengo unas raíces, algo de que agarrarme. Pero tú ... ¿tú de qué te agarras?

SHE: I hold on to you. I couldn't exist without you.

ELLA: But I wonder if I need you. Me pregunto si te necesito ... robándome la mitad de mis pensamientos, de mi tiempo, de mi sentir, de mis palabras ... como una sanguijuela!

SHE: I was unavoidable. You spawned me while you swam in that fish tank. It would take a long time to make me go away!

ELLA: Tú no eres tan importante. Ni tan fuerte. Unos meses, tal vez unos años, bajo el sol, y, ¡presto! ... desaparecerías. No quedaría ni rastro de ti. Yo soy la que existo. Yo soy la que soy. Tú ... no sé lo que eres.

SHE: But, if it weren't for me you would not be the one you are now. No serías la que eres. I gave yourself back to you. If I had not opened some doors and some windows for you, you would still be sitting in the dark, with your recuerdos, the idealized beaches of your childhood, and your rice and beans and the rest of your goddam obsolete memories! (*For the first time they face each other, furiously.*)

ELLA: Pero soy la más fuerte!

SHE: I am as strong as you are! (*With each line, they throw something at each other pillows, books, papers, etc.*)
ELLA: ¡Soy la más fuerte!
SHE: I am the strongest!
ELLA: ¡Te robaste parte de mí!
SHE: You wanted to be me once!
ELLA: ¡Estoy harta de ti!
SHE: Now you are!
ELLA: ¡Ojalá no estuvieras!
SHE: You can't get rid of me!
ELLA: ¡Alguien tiene que ganar!
SHE: No one shall win!

Loud sounds of sirens, shots, screams are heard outside. They run towards the window, then walk backwards in fear, speaking simultaneously.

SHE: They are shooting again!
ELLA: ¡Y están cortando los árboles!
SHE: They're poisoning the children in the schoolyard!
ELLA: ¡Y echando la basura y los muertos al río!
SHE: We're next! We're next!
ELLA: ¡Yo no salgo de aquí!
SHE: Let's get out of here! (*Another shot is heard. They look at each other.*)
ELLA: El mapa ...
SHE: Where's the map?

Black out.

Savings

A Musical Fable
1985

Savings

CHARACTERS

LEILA ZUKOV. The bank pianist. About 50.
MRS. GLORIA DOMÍNGUEZ. A Puerto Rican lady, about 48.
MRS. SYLVIA CABRERA. A Cuban lady, about 45.
LEROY YOUNG. A Black man, about 30.
MRS. BORESTEIN. A frail, gentle Jewish old lady, about 80.
FRED GONZÁLEZ. A Hispanic yuppie (young upward mobile professional) in his late 20s. A computer consultant.
MARCELLO MOFFETTI. The bank manager, about 59.
EDDIE RODRÍGUEZ. The mailman. Hispanic.
THE TELLERS. Two ladies of indeterminate age. These two actresses/singers will also play PEGGY CULPEPPER, a punk artist; MS. WONG, a neighbor; VICTORIA FRIBBLE, director of an aerobics exercise studio; JANE, her assistant; and a PARAMEDIC.

SET

The set consists of a piano, preferably a baby grand, surrounded by ten to twelve chairs with wheels. Some of these chairs will be occupied by mannequins when the action begins. The other mannequins will be placed on other chairs as the action progresses.

The backdrop should resemble the inside of a glass window at a bank. We can see part of the lettering backwards. There's a single door coming in from the street at stage right. At stage left there is the managers office. At stage right there are the tellers' windows. The windows are half-doors, which can open completely to allow tellers to step out.

There is also a front drop which resembles the bank as seen from the street. This drop has a see-through panel (the window) through which we can see the inside of the bank. This drop is used three times during the play.

TIME

OVERTURE: Sometime in the past.
ACT I covers the span of two days in the summer of 1985.
ACT II covers the next day.

PLACE

The lobby of a neighborhood savings bank where free piano concerts are offered every afternoon.

MUSICAL NUMBERS

ACT ONE

OVERTURE - Pianist
1. THERE GOES THE NEIGHBORHOOD - The Company
2. SUBTLETIES - Mofetti and Leila
3. TUTTI TOFUTTI - Tellers and Mailman
4. SAVINGS - Mrs. Borestein
5. IRON PUMPING WOMAN - Leroy
6. LEILA'S THEME - Leila
7. DEAR POSTMASTER GENERAL - Mailman
8. SONG TO LA VIRGEN - Mrs. Domínguez and Mrs. Cabrera

ACT TWO

9. GOOD AFTERNOON - Mofetti and Company
10. LEILA'S THEME (Reprise) - Leila and Company
11. GENTRIFICATION - Fred
12. LEILA AT NOONTIME - Mofetti
13. AEROBICS - Victoria Fribble and Assistant
14. MAKE ME BELIEVE - Leroy
15. ONE LAST SONG - Leila and Company
16. WE WON'T BE MOVED - Ms. Wong and Company

◇

Savings was first performed at INTAR Hispanic American Theater in New York City, on May 15, 1985 with the following cast:

LEILA ZUKOV .... D'Yan Forest
MARCELLO MOFETTI .... Lawrence Reed
FRED GONZÁLEZ .... Al Ferrer
SYLVIA CABRERA .... Georgia Gálvez
MRS. BORESTEIN .... Judith Granite
GLORIA DOMÍNGUEZ .... Carmen Rosario
MAILMAN .... Edward M. Rodríguez
LEROY YOUNG .... Peter Jay Fernández
TELLER 1,

PEGGY CULPEPPER,
VICTORIA FRIBBLE
and THE PARAMEDIC .... Marilyn Schnier
TELLER 2, JANE, MS. WONG ... Ricci Reyes Adán

It was directed by Max Ferrá. Music by Leon Odenz. Choreography by Frank Pietri.

OVERTURE

The front drop is down. We see the action from "outside" the bank. In the dark we hear the beginning of the overture. Slowly, a baby spot reveals LEILA *the pianist. She plays with passion and style. Immediately all the lights go up slowly and we see the bank customers sitting in various positions.* MRS. BORESTEIN *is lost in her memories,* FRED *is doing accounts in a small pocket calculator.* MRS. DOMÍNGUEZ *fans herself.* MRS. CABRERA *is a rapt listener.* LEROY *is distracted. The two* TELLERS *are behind their windows: one is filing her nails, the other one is reading a newspaper. As each customer speaks, he or she turns to his/her left or right and speaks to the dummy sitting there. Some of the speeches will overlap for a few lines at a time. Music plays throughout.*

FRED: ... for example, let's say you want to know into how many slices you should cut a banana so that you have one slice for each spoonful of cornflakes, you feed the information into the computer and it tells you exactly what to do ...

MRS. CABRERA: ... of course, I didn't play this type of music. (*Waves towards piano.*) Señora Carrillo, my piano teacher in Havana, taught me real classy music. My best piece was »Over the Waves».

LEROY: ... clothes make the man. You can't be too careful about the way you dress.

MRS. BORESTEIN: ... I couldn't remember the beginning or the end of my stories ... so, finally I decided not to go to Atlantic City after all ...

MRS. DOMÍNGUEZ: I used to own a botánica down the block ... herbs, images, holy water, all types of utensils for the believer. People are so desperate to believe, you know ... It was a good business. Then, they sold the building ...

MRS. CABRERA: ... my husband is a businessman. He owns "El Malecón Chino" down the block. The oldest Cuban-Chinese restaurant in this neighborhood ... He is Dominican. I taught him Cuban cuisine. The Chinese part he learned in Chinatown.

FRED: ... I bought it real cheap. I had my doubts about moving back to this neighborhood, but it is changing. And I am a businessman after all.

LEROY: ... I couldn't stand wearing the same clothes day in, day out, getting all messy walking in the jungle, killing people. Wearing those clothes didn't make me a man ...

MRS. DOMÍNGUEZ: ... I now live in the Bronx. Can't afford the rent here any longer. But I still come down for the concerts. I love music.

MRS. CABRERA: ... I haven't played the piano since I came here. The only keys I hit nowadays are those of the cash register at my husband's restaurant ...

MRS. BORESTEIN: ... Twenty-eight years I have been coming here. I don't come for the music. I come for the air conditioning in the summer and the heat in the winter. In the Spring I go to Atlantic City ...

At this point the musical overture should go into the beginning of the next song.

MRS. DOMÍNGUEZ Back in 1946, when my mother first opened the botánica down the block, some people said: "There goes the neighborhood. All this voodoo hoodoo at our doorsteps!"

TELLERS *begin the song stepping out of their booths. Later on everyone joins in, including* MR. MOFETTI *who comes out of his office and the* MAILMAN, *who enters from the street. This should have a choreography in which bank customers move the chairs around (their own and those with dummies on them).*

"THERE GOES THE NEIGHBORHOOD"

(Chorus)
VOODOO HOODOO
THERE GOES THE NEIGHBORHOODOO
VOODOO HOODOO
THERE GOES THE NEIGHBORHOODOO

BODEGAS, BAGEL SHOPS
BOTANICAS, SWEAT SHOPS
JUKE BOXES, RECORD SHOPS
DUCKTAILS AND HOT RODS

IT USED TO BE SO NICE
IT USED TO BE SO FINE
BUT SINCE THEY MOVED IN
WITH THEIR VOODOO HOODOO
SINCE THEY MOVED IN

THERE WENT THE NEIGHBORHOODOO

(Fred and Leroy)
REMEMBER WHEN THE GIRLS HUNG OUT AT THE CANDY STORE
DROOLING OVER EGG CREAMS AND COCA COLA

(Tellers)
THE BOYS THEY WANNA MARRY WERE OUT IN A PACK
THERE WAS NEVER ANY TIME TO GET THEM IN THE SACK

(Chorus)
VOODOO HOODOO
THERE GOES THE NEIGHBORHOODOO
VOODOO HOODOO
THERE GOES THE NEIGHBORHOODOO

(Leroy and Fred)
AND WHEN THE
CANDY MAN STOPPED
DELIVERING THE STUFF
THEN THE JUKE BOX SANG
OF SEX AND DRUGS
IN THE OLD CANDY STORE, YEAH, YEAH, YEAH
AT THE OLD CANDY STORE, YEAH, YEAH, YEAH
AT THE OLD CANDY …

(Chorus)
VOODOO HOODOO
THERE GOES THE NEIGHBORHOODOO
VOODOO HOODOO
THERE GOES THE NEIGHBORHOODOO

BEATLES, HEAD SHOPS
MARCHES AT THE BUS STOP
GURUS, MANTRAS
ELECTRIC SECOND HAND SHOPS
IT USED TO BE SO NICE
IT USED TO BE SO FINE
BUT SINCE THEY MOVED IN
WITH THEIR VOODOO HOODOO

SINCE THEY MOVED IN
THERE WENT THE NEIGHBORHOODOO

(Fred)
I'D RATHER MEDITATE
I'D RATHER CONTEMPLATE
I'D RATHER MAKE LOVE ALL NIGHT LONG
A GIRL BURNT HER BRA
A BOY BURNT THE FLAG
ON TOP OF THE COUNTER AT THE OLD CANDY
STORE

(Chorus)
VOODOO HOODOO
THERE GOES THE NEIGHBORHOODOO
VOODOO HOODOO
THERE GOES THE NEIGHBORHOODOO

BLACKS AND WHITE
JEWS AND GENTILES
HINDUS, KRAUTS
SPICKS AND ORIENTILES

THIS BARRIO USED TO BE
A DANDY NEIGHBORHOOD
BUT SINCE THEY MOVED IN
WITH THEIR VOODOO HOODOO
SINCE THEY MOVED IN
THERE WENT THE NEIGHBORHOODOO

(Leroy)
AFTER THE BLAST WAS PAST
AND WE WERE LEFT ALONE
TO PICK AND SHOVEL
TO RIFF AND RAFF
TO CLEAN THE STREET WITH OUR BACK
AGAIN THEY ARE SAYIN' HOOOOOOOOOO

(Chorus)
VOODOO HOODOO
THERE GOES THE NEIGHBORHOODOO
VOODOO HOODOO
THERE GOES THE NEIGHBORHOODOO

IT GOT VERY STRANGE
YOU SAW DIFF'RENT COLORS
HEARD DIFF'RENT SOUNDS
YOU SMELLED DIFF'RENT ODORS
IT USED TO BE SO NICE
IT USED TO BE SO FINE
BUT SINCE THEY MOVED IN—
WITH THEIR VOODOO HOODOO
SINCE THEY MOVED IN—

Everyone exits. Black out. End of overture.

ACT ONE

When lights come up it is another day. There are only three dummies sitting in various chairs on both sides of the piano. Only LEILA *is on stage, standing by the piano arranging her sheet of music.* MOFETTI *opens the door of his office, sticks his head out, looks right and left, sneaks up behind* LEILA.

MOFETTI: (*Smelling her ear.*) Hmmm!
LEILA: (*Startled.*) Marcello! Have you gone crazy?
MOFETTI: Long ago.
LEILA: You used to be more careful.
MOFETTI: I still am. It was just an impulse. It must be the heat.
LEILA: It is 50 degrees in here.
MOFETTI: You used to be more romantic than that.
LEILA: That was last year.
MOFETTI: What's wrong with this year?
LEILA: I don't get to see you as often.
MOFETTI: You see me every day. I see you every day.
LEILA: You know what I mean.
MOFETTI: We've been over this before, haven't we?
LEILA: Yes, we have. Still, I prefer last year. And the one before.
MOFETTI: Nothing's changed for me.
LEILA: That's easy for you to say.
MOFETTI: Leila, I never deceived you. We both have been very clear about this since the very beginning, remember?
LEILA: I remember what I said then ... (LEILA *plays and begins the song.*)

"SUBTLETIES"

LEILA:
I'M ACCESSIBLE
I'M OBTAINABLE
IF YOU WANT ME
YOU CAN HAVE ME
I AM READY
I AM WILLING
I AM ABLE
I'M AVAILABLE

IF YOU WANT ME
YOU CAN TOUCH ME
YOU CAN KISS ME
I'M AVAILABLE

MOFETTI:
SHE THINKS
I'M IRRESISTIBLE
I FIND SHE'S
IRREPRESSIBLE
IF MY WIFE MABEL
SHOULD FIND OUT
SHE'D THINK I'M
SO CONTEMPTIBLE
BUT WHAT CAN I DO
IF SHE SAYS
SHE'S AVAILABLE

LEILA:
IF YOU WANT TO
YOU CAN TOUCH ME

MOFETTI:
I CAN KISS HER
I CAN HAVE HER

LEILA:
THERE'S NO TIME TO WASTE AT TWILIGHT
WHEN DARKNESS IS DUE TO ARRIVE

MOFETTI:

IT WAS A CONVENIENT ARRANGEMENT
BECAUSE WE WERE HARDLY ALIVE

LEILA:
I'M ACCESSIBLE
I'M OBTAINABLE
IF YOU WANT ME
YOU CAN HAVE ME
I AM READY
I AM WILLING
I AM ABLE
I'M AVAILABLE

MOFETTI:
SHE THINKS
I'M IRRESISTIBLE
I FIND SHE'S
IRREPRESSIBLE
IF MY WIFE MABEL
SHOULD FIND OUT
SHE'D THINK I'M
SO CONTEMPTIBLE
BUT WHAT CAN I DO
IF SHE SAYS
SHE'S AVAILABLE

BOTH:
IT'S UNROMANTIC
UNACCEPTABLE
BUT WE KEPT COMPANY
EARLY EVENINGS
WE MADE MUSIC
BEFORE THE RUSH HOUR
'CAUSE WE WERE WILLING
ABLE
LONELY
READY
AND AVAILABLE

After the song FRED *enters.* MOFETTI *goes towards his office.*

FRED: Good morning, Mr. Mofetti.
MOFETTI: Good morning, Mr. González.
FRED: I wonder if you have a moment. I've been meaning to talk to you about this new line of computers I'm representing.
MOFETTI: Maybe some other time. I have a lot of work to do right now.
FRED: I'm glad you said that. Because precisely that's my point. With this computer you won't have so much work to do. It will practically manage the bank all by itself.
MOFETTI: Thanks, Fred, I like my work. Besides, don't you know what our motto is "People to People Banking." Have a good day. (MOFETTI *goes into his office.*)

FRED: (FRED, *without missing a beat, turns to* LEILA.) How about you, Ms. Zukov?

LEILA: Oh, Fred, what would I do with a computer?

FRED: You mean you haven't heard about the new Japanese Computer Piano?

LEILA: Heaven forbid!

FRED: Ms. Zukov, you have to look ahead—into the future. You are not going to be playing the piano at this bank forever.

LEILA: Why not?

FRED: Well, for one, this bank may not be here much longer. The neighborhood is changing.

LEILA: This bank will always be here. This neighborhood has changed many times before and people always continued to save money.

FRED: The building may be sold.

LEILA: The Walenska family will never do that.

FRED: Who are they?

LEILA: The owners.

FRED: A "mom and pop" bank! That kind of business is going the way of the hoola hoop. I insist you should think about that computer piano.

MRS. CABRERA: (*Entering.*) Good morning.

LEILA and FRED: Good morning, Mrs. Cabrera.

FRED: (MRS. CABRERA *sits down next to a dummy. She looks at it and nods hello.* FRED *sits next to her.*) Mrs. Cabrera, I was thinking ...

MRS. CABRERA: No. (*To* LEILA.) Are you starting soon, Leila? I have to get back to the restaurant ... we are short of help today.

LEILA: As soon as more people come in.

FRED: (MRS. BORESTEIN *enters from the street. She walks slowly, aided by a cane.* FRED *gets up and helps her to her seat.*) Mrs. Borestein, here, let me help you. How are you today?

MRS. BORESTEIN: Thank you, Leroy. I am fine. How are you? (MRS. BORESTEIN *sits on the other side of the dummy.*)

FRED: Fred. I'm Fred.

MRS. BORESTEIN: Of course you are.

FRED: Have you thought about our conversation?

MRS. BORESTEIN: I don't think I'll be going to Atlantic City this week.

FRED: No. I mean about the computer. The word processor, for your novels.

MRS. BORESTEIN: Ah, that. I gave up writing long ago. I kept forgetting the plot.

FRED: Precisely. With a computer you won't have that problem. It will remember for you . . .

MRS. BORESTEIN: Nobody reads books anymore.

FRED: Romantic novels are selling very well in the supermarkets nowadays. Now is the time for you to get back in the business. And with a computer . . .

MRS. DOMÍNGUEZ: (MRS. DOMÍNGUEZ *Entering.*) Hello, everybody. (*Sits down, exhausted.*)

MRS. CABRERA: Hi, Sylvia, you look bushed.

MRS. DOMÍNGUEZ: That subway was like a furnace.

FRED: In this weather you should take the bus.

MRS. DOMÍNGUEZ: From the Bronx? What I really would like to do is move back here. It was so easy living down the street.

FRED: Why don't you move back?

MRS. DOMÍNGUEZ: For the same reason I moved out. I can't afford it.

MAILMAN: (*The* MAILMAN *enters. In a booming voice, from the door.*) Mailman!

LEILA: Hello, Eddie, Mofetti was asking for you.

MAILMAN: I'm sure it isn't the mail he's expecting from me. (*Calling out.*) Mr. Mofetti!

MOFETTI: (MOFETTI *comes out of his office.*) Hi, Eddie, what's new?

MAILMAN: (*Handing* MOFETTI *a pack of letters.*) What's new? (*Gets closer to* MOFETTI. *Confidentially.*) If I were you, Mr. Mofetti, I'd put all my dough on "Pretty Feet."

MOFETTI: That horse hasn't won a race in months! What else is new?

MAILMAN: (*Thinking.*) What else is new? . . . Hmmm . . . Oh, yes! You mean you haven't seen it?

MOFETTI: Seen what?

MAILMAN: They've just put up the sign.

MRS. CABRERA: What sign?

MAILMAN: You'll never guess what it is.

FRED: What?

MAILMAN: The new store.

MRS. DOMÍNGUEZ: You mean the one where my botánica used to be?

MAILMAN: That one. You'll never guess what it is!

FRED: An arts and crafts boutique?

LEILA: Can't be. There are already three of those on the block.

MRS. CABRERA: I hope it is a bodega. Since "Mi Tierra" closed I have to walk five blocks to the supermarket. And they don't even have yuca there.

MAILMAN: No, it's not a bodega. It is "Tutti-Tofutti – Health Restaurant and Salad Bar."

MRS. CABRERA: Tutti what?

FRED: Tofutti. It is a non-dairy ice cream. Made from beans.

MRS. CABRERA: (*Scandalized.*) From beans! ¡Qué barbaridad! What are they doing to OUR food!

MRS. DOMÍNGUEZ: And in MY botánica!

MRS. CABRERA: Tafetta, you say?

MRS. BORESTEIN: I had a dress like that. Dark green it was ... Dark green tafetta ... with ruffles. It was long, a gown ... for parties and occasions.

LEROY: (LEROY *enters eating toffutti.*) Yo! Have you seen what they just opened next to the "Vade Retro" Gallery?

MAILMAN: TOFUTTI!

TELLER 1: (TELLERS *stick their heads out of their windows and sing in harmony.*) TOFUTTI!

TELLER 2: TOFUTTI!

LEROY: Yeah! And they're giving away free samples!

Music begins. TELLERS *come out of their booths and sing along with the* MAILMAN.)

"TUTTI-TOFUTTI"

SAY ADIÓS TO CUCHIFRITOS
SAY CIAO TO CALZONES
SAY SHALOM TO KNISHES
KEEP YOUR CHOLESTEROL DOWN
KEEP YOUR WAIST TRIM AND SEXY
THERE'S NOTHING IN THE WORLD LIKE ...

TUTTI TOFUTTI
TUTTI TOFUTTI
THERE'S NOTHING
LIKE TOFUTTI
GIVE ME A SCOOP
GIVE ME TWO
I NEED A COLD FIX
I NEED TO FEEL GOOD
TUTTI TOFUTTI

TUTTI TOFUTTI
NOTHING LIKE TOFUTTI

IT LOOKS KIND OF FUNNY
IT DON'T TASTE LIKE MUCH
BUT ITS GOOD FOR YOU
AND MAKES YOU LIVE LONGER

IT COSTS A FEW PENNIES
IT HAS NO LACTOSE
BUT IT FEEDS YOU WELL
AND MAKES YOU LOOK BETTER

TUTTI TOFUTTI I LOVE
TUTTI TOFUTTI
THERE'S NOTHING IN THE WORLD
LIKE TOFUTTI
GIVE ME A SCOOP
GIVE ME TWO
I NEED A COLD FIX
I NEED TO FEEL GOOD

TUTTI TOFUTTI I LOVE
TUTTI TOFUTTI
THERE'S NOTHING IN THE WORLD
LIKE TOFUTTI

The TELLERS *and the* MAILMAN *exit through the street door, followed by* FRED, MRS. CABRERA AND MRS. DOMÍNGUEZ.

MRS. DOMÍNGUEZ: (*Exiting.*) Come on, let's get some!

MRS. CABRERA: (*Following* MRS. DOMÍNGUEZ.) I gotta try this tafetta . . .

FRED: Anything for free!

LEROY: (*After they leave,* LEROY *stands up and addresses* MOFETTI.) Mr. Mofetti, I wonder if I could have a word with you. Private.

MOFETTI: Sure, come into my office.

MRS. BORESTEIN: (*To herself.*) . . . I think it was blue. Blue tafetta . . . low cut . . . (*She turns to the dummy sitting next to her. Music begins.*) I wore it the first time David took me to Atlantic City . . . I have a picture right here. (*Pulls out an old perfumed soap box from her purse, opens it and fingers some of its contents. Pulls out a photograph, shows it to dummy.*) ... David and I used to walk for hours, up and down the boardwalk ... under my parasol ... (*Puts picture back. Takes out bank book, flips through the pages.*) Maybe at the end of the year I'll have enough saved to go back there ... (*She puts bank book inside box. She sings:*)

"SAVINGS"

PUT A DIME AWAY
FOR A RAINY DAY
SAVE YOUR MEMORIES
PUT IT ALL INSIDE
IN THAT LITTLE BOX
THE ONE HE GAVE YOU
FULL OF PERFUMED SOAP
THAT VALENTINE'S DAY
IN NINETEEN FORTY-EIGHT

PUT A DIME AWAY
FOR A RAINY DAY
TO BUY A BOTTLE OF WINE
WITH YOUR LIFE'S SAVINGS
THAT FIT IN A BOX
THE ONE HE GAVE YOU
FULL OF PERFUMED SOAP
THAT VALENTINE'S DAY
BACK IN NINETEEN FORTY-EIGHT

WHEN YOU ARE ALL ALONE
WAITING FOR A CHECK
THAT WON'T PAY THE BILLS
PILING UP IN THAT BOX
THE ONE HE GAVE YOU
BACK IN NINETEEN FORTY-EIGHT

PUT A DIME AWAY
FOR A RAINY DAY
HOPING TO MAKE A DIFFERENCE
WHEN NO ONE WILL CARE
IF YOU'RE STILL ALIVE
INSIDE A LITTLE BOX
THE ONE HE GAVE YOU

THAT VALENTINE'S DAY
BACK IN NINETEEN FORTY-EIGHT

MRS. BORESTEIN *continues to look inside her box. Lights go up.* LEROY *enters from* MOFETTI'*s office. He looks dejected, sits next to* MRS. BORESTEIN. *She looks at him, returning to reality.*

MRS. BORESTEIN: Today is a different day, isn't it?

LEROY: Yes, it is. But tomorrow ... tomorrow will really be more different, Mrs. B.

MRS. BORESTEIN: Most of the time one day is no different than the next.

LEROY: Not for me. Tomorrow I won't have a place to live in.

MRS. BORESTEIN: What happened, Fred?

LEROY: I'm Leroy.

MRS. BORESTEIN: Of course you are. What happened, son?

LEROY: I got the final notice a couple of days ago. I have to leave by tomorrow. I knew this was going to happen when the building was sold. Since then, the new owner has been harassing the tenants to get us out. I've been trying to get some money to move, but, no way ... everything is so expensive.

MRS. BORESTEIN: Have you thought about Atlantic City?

LEROY: No, Mrs. B, I haven't. I like this city and I'd like to stay here. In fact, I'd like to stay in that apartment. I've lived there for eight years, I've put a lot of work in it.

MRS. BORESTEIN: Where are you going to sleep?

LEROY: Where to sleep is the least of my problems. There's always the subway, the streets, Grand Central Station. The problem is, where will I hang all my clothes? Shopping bags won't do.

MRS. BORESTEIN: Don't you have any relatives?

LEROY: Not here.

MRS. BORESTEIN: Atlantic City is such a nice place.

LEROY: Mrs. B, Atlantic City is not what it used to be. I've told you before. Now it is a gambling resort. It is full of casinos, chorus girls ...

MRS. BORESTEIN: (*Ignoring* LEROY'*s words.*) David and I used to take our constitutional along the boardwalk every evening.

LEROY: Mrs. B ... (*To himself, giving up.*) Ah, why spoil her memories.

MRS. BORESTEIN: Here, let me show you (*Pulls out another photograph from her box and shows it to* LEROY.) That's

David. Guess who that one is? (MRS. BORESTEIN *has shown this picture to* LEROY *many times before, but he always makes believe it is the first time he sees it.* LEILA *watches the action.*)

LEROY: This beautiful lady here? Who could that be? She looks like a movie star to me!

LEILA: (*From the piano.*) Let me see that.

MRS. BORESTEIN: (LEROY *goes over to the piano with photograph.* MRS BORESTEIN *gets up and goes towards the piano too.*) I'm the one with the hat.

LEILA: You look beautiful, Mrs. Borestein.

LEROY: And look at Mr. Borestein! That white suit!

LEILA *plays "Savings" reprise.* MRS. BORESTEIN *sings.*

... FULL OF PERFUMED SOAP
THAT VALENTINE'S DAY
BACK IN 1948 ...

The three remain there looking at photographs throughout the following scene. FRED *enters from the street with* PEGGY CULPEPPER, *the punk rocker. They are both eating Tofutti. They are in the middle of a conversation. They stand behind a line of dummies in front of the cashier's window.*

PEGGY: ... all this thing about beauty is a load of shit. Who said art has to be beautiful? I sing about ugliness. About everyday life ugly things. I know they are ugly. Ugly is ugly and we should learn to appreciate it ... Oh, my God! Look at this line!

FRED: How do you describe what you do?

PEGGY: I am a minimal retro avant garde expressionist singer. That's what my boyfriend Julian says.

FRED: I see.

PEGGY: I sing Saturdays at the Scum Club. It is around the corner, you know.

FRED: Yes, I've seen it.

PEGGY: (*Impatient.*) This line is always the same! It sucks ... and I have to cash this check. I gotta get more garbage bags.

FRED: Spring cleaning?

PEGGY: Naw, they are for a new sculpture.

FRED: Are you a sculptor too?

PEGGY: No, Julian is. I help him at the gallery—the Vade Retro. You've seen it, next to the new Tofutti. It used to be in SoHo, but he couldn't afford the rent there anymore. I think the same thing is gonna happen here—for sure ... Are you new around here too?

FRED: Yes. And no. I live here now. I bought a house a while back. Real cheap. I just finished fixing it up. I live on the top floor. My office is on the ground floor. The rest I rent. Real expensive. But I used to live in this neighborhood a long time ago.

PEGGY: Ah. I'm from California. It was too pretty for me, ya know. I love it here. But, it's changing. I moved here because it was so different, ya know. Different people, like wow, different things. Now almost everybody looks like me. (*Impatient, looking towards* TELLERS' *windows.*) What are they doing in there! They are so slow!

FRED: Humans are useless for this kind of work. They should be fired and replaced with Lizzie.

PEGGY: Who's she?

FRED: It is a computer. Very efficient, very fast.

PEGGY: (*Dumb.*) Ah.

FRED: I'm a computer consultant. Here's my card. I also sell them. Could I interest you in one maybe?

PEGGY: Naw. They're not ugly enough ... (*Looking at the line.*) This is too much! Like, ya know, I can't wait any longer. I'll come back later. (PEGGY *turns to leave.* FRED *follows her.*)

FRED: I'll walk you back to the Gallery ... (*Exiting.*) "Vade Retro"—that's a good name.

PEGGY: Julian read it somewhere, ya know, like a a book or something. (FRED *and* PEGGY *exit.*)

LEROY: (*Holding a photograph.*) That was a nice apartment you and Mr. David had.

LEILA: (*Taking the photograph.*) Yes. They don't make them like that anymore.

MRS. BORESTEIN: I lived there before I met him. He just moved in.

LEROY: Smart move.

MRS. BORESTEIN: (*Going back to her seat.*) That's what you should do: find yourself a nice girlfriend with an apartment.

LEROY: Easier said than done. I've given up on girlfriends, Mrs. B.

MRS. BORESTEIN: Don't say that, Leroy. You never know whom you are going to meet tomorrow.

LEROY: Whom? I already met her. But it isn't working out—she's too busy working out ... I met her at a gym where I used to hang out. The most beautiful Puerto Rican lady you ever saw. She was born in the South Bronx, but if you ask her, she always says "I'm from Ponce." She assured me she was a direct descendant from the Taíno Indians. She showed me her teeth—shovel shaped incisos. That's the sign of the Indian, she says. She paid attention to me for a while because I was a musician. And everybody loves a serenade. I sang under her window for many a night. I fell in love with her, but she was already in love with someone else. A married someone else. She's been waiting for this guy for ten years. Can you imagine, Mrs. B? Ten years!

LEILA: I can imagine! (*Music begins.*)

MRS. BORESTEIN: How can she stand it?

LEROY: I told you. She lifts weights. (LEROY *sings:*)

"IRON PUMPING WOMAN"

IRON PUMPING WOMAN
WITH SHOVEL-SHAPED INCISORS
DOUBLE-PIERCED EARS
AND HIGH-STRUNG EMOTIONS
LONG LOVING WOMAN
WITH ONE-MOUTHFUL BREASTS
HONEY-COLORED EYES
AND TONGUE OF SUGAR

IRON PUMPING WOMAN
RUNNING IN THE PARK
DRINKING UP A RIVER
CRYING UP A STORM

LONG LOVING WOMAN
WAITING BY THE PHONE
CAN'T HEAR MY MUSIC
CANT' HEAR MY SONG

SWEET AND SOFT WOMAN
PUMPING IRON ON A THOUGHT

CHASING TIME BEATING HEART
SWEET TOUGH LADY HOW YOU SWEAT

IRON PUMPING WOMAN
TRYING TO FORGET
HOW LONELY ARE YOUR NIGHTS
HOW COLD IS YOUR BED

LONG ARMS WITH BIG HANDS
HOLDING ON TO THE WIND
IRON PUMPING WOMAN
IRON PUMPING WOMAN
PUMPING IRON
AND BUTTERFLIES.

Black out.

When lights come up again it is another day. Only LEILA *is on stage playing. Another two dummies occupy two more chairs.)*

MOFETTI: (*Entering from his office.*) Leila, I must speak to you. (LEILA *ignores him, continues playing.*)

MOFETTI: It is important.

LEILA: (*She stops playing.*) How important?

MOFETTI: Very.

LEILA: I waited for you all night.

MOFETTI: I thought so. I'm sorry. I was at a meeting with the bank's president. I couldn't get to a phone. Afterwards, I was so upset . . .

LEILA: What's going on, Marcello?

MOFETTI: Plenty, Leila. Plenty. (*He walks around the piano, sits on the stool next to* LEILA.) I don't know how to tell you. I don't know how to tell any one.

LEILA: Try me.

MOFETTI: Leila . . . it's all over!

LEILA: What? What is over? . . . You mean . . . us . . . our . . .

MOFETTI: Yes, that. Everything. I saw it coming, but now it is final . . . The bank is closing. (LEILA *begins to play a very sad melody.* MOFETTI *listens for a while with head bowed.*) I know how you feel. But . . . how do you think I feel? (*Stands up.*) I've worked here all my life. It took me years to be promoted to manager. I don't know how to do anything else. At my age, where am I going to get another job? And I'm not ready for retirement yet! I'm full of vigor, you know that.

LEILA: (LEILA *stops playing. Gives him a look.*) Is the bank losing money?

MOFETTI: No.

LEILA: It doesn't have enough customers?

MOFETTI: It has enough.

LEILA: Then, why is it closing?

MOFETTI: They are selling the building. The Walenskas have been offered a deal they can't refuse. Also, they feel the bank can't compete with the giants.

LEILA: What will happen with the building?

MOFETTI: Well, the five floors above will be turned into luxury condominiums. Here, in the bank, there will be a Victoria Fribble Dancercise Studio.

LEILA: Victoria Fribble! In this neighborhood?

MOFETTI: It is changing, Leila. And changing fast. Can't you tell? There's no future for this type of bank here.

LEILA: (*Pause.* LEILA *plays same sad melody again.*) What will happen to us?

MOFETTI: I don't know. We have to figure things out. I have to think.

LEILA: (*They think.* LEILA *plays some more.*) There isn't really much to think about, is there? I mean, you are married. You have a wife, children, grandchildren, a dog and a house in New Jersey. You are not going to commute just to see me, are you?

MOFETTI: I don't know ... there are practical aspects to the situation ... I have to consider ...

LEILA: Let's not fool ourselves. We were a convenience to each other. Yet ...

MOFETTI: (*Almost to himself.*) Yes, it was convenient ... I mean, no, I ... Leila, we have been seeing each other for twelve years. I hear you play every day ... I'm going to miss you.

LEILA: I will miss you too, Marcello.

MOFETTI: (LEILA *plays.* MOFETTI *is thoughtful.*) I remember when you started to play here. You brought happiness to this bank. We got a lot of new customers because of you. What's more important: you brought ME happiness.

MOFETTI *Kisses the top of* LEILA*'s head and exits to his office.* LEILA *stares ahead in a daze.* LEILA *sings:*

"LEILA'S THEME"

WHEN I WAS YOUNG I WANTED
TO MAKE THE WORLD LAUGH
WHEN I WAS YOUNG I THOUGHT
I COULD MAKE THE WORLD DANCE
WHEN I WAS YOUNG I DANCED
AND LAUGHED AND SANG
I THOUGHT I WAS THE WORLD
ONCE WHEN I WAS YOUNG

LIFE IS A BOWL OF CHERRIES
LIFE IS A CABARET
UNDER THE FULL MOON
ROWING ON THE LAKE
HAPPY SHOOTING THE BREEZE

I PAID NO INCOME TAXES
I WAS A VAUDEVILLE STAR
I HAD A LOVER IN EVERY TOWN
MY HAIR WAS REALLY BLONDE

PERHAPS IT WAS LACK OF TALENT
PERHAPS IT WAS LACK OF LUCK
BUT I DON'T REALLY CARE
I HAVE NO REGRETS
I NEVER MADE IT TO CARNEGIE HALL

LIFE IS A BOWL OF CHERRIES
LIFE IS CABARET
OVER THE RAINBOW
PLAYING THE SAME SONGS
I'M NOW LOSING THE GAME

I TRIED TO BE A WINNER
I DREAMT OF THE HEIGHTS OF FAME
I WANTED LOVE FOREVER
MY DREAMS DID NOT COME TRUE

PERHAPS IT WAS ALL MY FAULT
PERHAPS IT WAS NOT MY DOING
BUT I CAN'T REALLY SAY
I HAVE NO REGRETS
I NEVER WON THE ACADEMY AWARD

LIFE IS A BOWL OF CHERRIES
LIFE IS A CABARET
UNDER THE FULL MOON
ROWING ON THE LAKE ...

WHEN I WAS YOUNG I THOUGHT
I COULD MAKE THE WORLD LAUGH
WHEN I WAS YOUNG I THOUGHT
I COULD MAKE THE WORLD DANCE

LEILA *stops and cries. Dabs her eyes with a tissue, then wipes the piano keys with it.* LEROY *enters.*

LEROY: Miss Leila ... ? Are you all right?

LEILA: I'm fine ... thank you ...

LEROY: Forgive me, Miss L, but you don't look too fine to me.

LEILA: (*Trying to control herself.*) ... It's nothing ... nothing ... just ... life ...

LEROY: (*Sitting next to* LEILA *on the piano stool.*) Come on, then ... cheer up! Life is a bowl of cherries ... remember? You always say that.

LEILA: I do, don't I? You know what it is, Leroy, when you sing the same old songs over and over, like I do? I guess you come to believe the words, the ideas they express, even if they have nothing to do with reality. (LEILA *tries to smile, but ends up crying.*)

LEROY: I've never seen you like this, Miss Leila ... I bet it is that Mofetti!

LEILA: It isn't really his fault ... it was an offer they couldn't refuse. (LEILA *plays her theme. Up part.* LEROY *stops her.*)

LEROY: What offer? Who couldn't refuse? What are you talking about?

LEILA: I'm sure Mofetti will tell everyone later. It is the bank ... it's going out of business.

LEROY: (*Gets up thoroughly confused.*) Out of business? No, no, it can't be. When?

LEILA: Very soon. A few days, a few weeks ... I don't know ...

LEROY: (*Somewhat agitated, to himself.*) Then ... then ... there's no time to waste. I gotta get moving. (LEROY *exits hurriedly.*)

MAILMAN: (*Entering from the street. He's about to announce his presence with his usual operatic "Mailman" when* LEROY *runs into him, punching all the air out of the surprised*

MAILMAN. *Catching his breath.*) He used to like me. What's wrong with him? Did he finally go crazy?

LEILA: I think everybody is finally going crazy here today, Eddie.

MAILMAN: It can't be crazier than down at the post office.

LEILA: But at least the post office will always be there. It must be reassuring to work in a place like that—solid, stable ... an institution, like the Rock of Gibraltar.

MAILMAN: It is more like a rock around your neck. You can't imagine what it is like in there, Miss Zukov. I'm fed up with the whole thing. I wrote a letter to the Postmaster General. I hope to hear from him soon.

LEILA: What did you write to him about?

MAILMAN *sings:*

"DEAR POSTMASTER GENERAL"

DEAR POSTMASTER GENERAL
DEAR POSTMASTER GENERAL
YOUR PICTURE HANGS ON THE WALL
NEXT TO OUR PRESIDENT
I FEEL I KNOW YOU AFTER ALL
AND I WANT TO SAY I'M NOT CONTENT
BUT
DOWN AT THE POST
DOWN AT THE POST
THEY JUST KEEP THROWIN' THE MAIL
DOWN AT THE POST
DOWN AT THE POST
THEY JUST KEEP THROWIN' THE MAIL

DEAR POSTMASTER GENERAL
DEAR POSTMASTER GENERAL
I BRING THE LETTERS IN A FLASH
I BRING GOOD NEWS AND BAD NEWS AND LOVE
NOTES
I BRING BILLS TO PAY CHECKS TO CASH
EVEN JUNK MAIL I CAREFULLY TOTE
BUT WHAT CAN YOU DO?
DO YOU REALLY CARE?
THAT
PACKAGES GET LOST
LINES ARE TOO LONG
STAMPS WITHOUT GLUE

ZIP CODES ARE NO GOOD!
AND WHY WHY OH WHY ARE THE CLERKS
ALWAYS IN SUCH A BAD MOOD?

DEAR POSTMASTER GENERAL
DEAR POSTMASTER GENERAL
I DON'T MIND THE DOG BITES
I DON'T MIND THE SNOW, THE SLEET
THE RAIN, THE FOG, THE GLOOM OF NIGHT
THE PAIN IN THE SOLE OF MY FEET
BUT
DOWN AT THE POST
DOWN AT THE POST
THEY JUST KEEP THROWIN' THE MAIL
DOWN AT THE POST
DOWN AT THE POST
THEY JUST KEEP THROWIN'
KEEP THROWIN' THE MAIL.
YOURS RESPECTFULLLY, EDDIE RODR/'IGUEZ.

MAILMAN: (*To* MOFETTI *entering from his office.*) Good afternoon, Mr. Mofetti. Here's your mail.
MOFETTI: Thank you, Eddie.
MAILMAN: Don't mention it. It is always a pleasure to deliver mail here.
MOFETTI: Don't you have any suggestions today?
MAILMAN: What's the use? The OTB Parlor closed today. I hear Häagen-Dazs ice cream is moving in there. I guess we'll have to bet on the Swiss Almond Vanilla. Well, have a good day.
LEILA: Goodbye, Eddie. And good luck with your letter. (MAILMAN *tips his hat and exits.*)
MOFETTI: Leila, about what we talked before ...
LEILA: Yes?
MOFETTI: I'd like to ask you a favor ... Please don't say anything to the customers about the bank closing. I ...
LEILA: Don't say anything?!
MOFETTI: ... Just for the moment. I ...
LEILA: But, Marcello, why?
MOFETTI: I need some time ... to prepare myself. To think.
LEILA: To think? About what? It is not fair to the customers. They should know what's happening.
MOFETTI: (*Edgy.*) I'll tell them tomorrow.

LEILA: Today, tomorrow ... what's the difference!
MOFETTI: I'm making some calls, talking to some people ...
LEILA: (*Hopeful.*) You think ... you think there may be a chance? That something can be done?
MOFETTI: I doubt it, but ...
LEILA: Have you talked to anybody who knows about these things?
MOFETTI: Like who?
LEILA: ... like ... Tina Wong ...
MOFETTI: What does she know? A young attorney, just starting out.
LEILA: She's very bright. I hear she's now with the Chinatown Legal Services. Why don't you call her?
MOFETTI: What for? What can she do? Is she going to get me a few million dollars to buy the bank?
LEILA: There may be other options.
MOFETTI: I have to think about it.
LEILA: Think, think! All you do is think! You are so wishy-washy, Marcello! You just can't make a decision, face the consequences. Like that time you said you'd think about a divorce. How long ago was that? Can you remember?
MOFETTI: It's not that easy. One has to consider every angle of a situation.
MRS. CABRERA and MRS. DOMÍNGUEZ: (*Entering together from the street.*) Good afternoon.
LEILA and MOFETTI: Good afternoon. (MRS. CABRERA *and* MRS. DOMÍNGUEZ *sit down.* MOFETTI *turns to leave.* LEILA *follows him to his office.*)
LEILA: (*Whispering, angry.*) Well, if you don't call Tina Wong, I will.
MOFETTI: (*Breathing deep.*) Do whatever you want. It's useless, anyway. (*They both enter* MOFETTI'*s office, arguing and whispering, closing the door behind them.*)
MRS. DOMÍNGUEZ: Hmmm ... I wonder what's going ...
MRS. CABRERA: (*Distracted.*) Where?
MRS. DOMÍNGUEZ: With Mr. Mofetti and Leila.
MRS. CABRERA: (*Uninterested.*) The same thing that's been going on for twelve years.
MRS. DOMÍNGUEZ: (*Opening her eyes in disbelief.*) You mean ... the two of them? ... Nooo! I can't believe it! You never told me!
MRS. CABRERA: You must be blind. I thought everyone knew.
MRS. DOMÍNGUEZ: I didn't know. I didn't even notice! ... I guess I am not into bochinche as much as I used to ...

Ah, I think I'm getting old ... You know ... this morning I almost got mugged in the subway. Forty years living in New York and it had never happened to me! I was always so alert.

MRS. CABRERA: I don't know why you put up with all this. You have a house in Puerto Rico, why don't you go back?

MRS. DOMÍNGUEZ: I did once. After José passed away. We had struggled so hard for so many years to save money to buy that house in Guayama. It was the dream we came here with. I went back but stayed only three months. I couldn't get used to living there again. I missed New York. Isn't that crazy? (*She realizes* MRS. CABRERA *is not listening*) ... Sylvia ... you haven't heard a word I said! What's wrong with you today!

MRS. CABRERA: Ay, Gloria vieja, I couldn't sleep a wink last night. Jacinto kept me up all night.

MRS. DOMÍNGUEZ: (*Laughing.*) Ho, ho ... the old devil!

MRS. CABRERA: Not that! Jacinto is so worried. The landlord is raising the rent of the restaurant. A three hundred percent increase!

MRS. DOMÍNGUEZ: Virgen del Carmen!

MRS. CABRERA: And now he blames himself for not buying the building ten years ago. He could have bought it for a song. But he said running a restaurant was enough of a headache. He thought the price was high. But most of all, he didn't want to owe so much money to the bank. Do you know that he handles everything in cash?

MRS. DOMÍNGUEZ: Ay, m'ija! In this country unless you owe money to somebody, you are a nobody.

MRS. CABRERA: Now he's dying of regret. And I have to bite my tongue. I told him to buy that building. For the future, for our children. He said, "I don't want my children living in this lousy neighborhood." Well, look whose children are moving here now. (*Points to dummies.*) They can afford to pay $1500 a month for a closet and a bathroom.

LEILA *enters from the manager's office dabbing her eyes with a tissue. She sits at the piano and cleans the keyboard with the same tissue.*

MRS. DOMÍNGUEZ: Maybe he can raise the price of food to make up for the difference in rent.

MRS. CABRERA: Ay, Gloria, who's going to pay $15 for a plate of rice and beans? ... I don't know what we're going to do!

MRS. DOMÍNGUEZ: I'll tell you what. Take this. (*Takes out of her bag a manila envelope.*) When you pay the rent this month put some of these leaves in the envelope, together with the check.

MRS. CABRERA: Do you think that will help?

MRS. DOMÍNGUEZ: That, and a good prayer.

Music begins. MRS. DOMÍNGUEZ *and* MRS. CABRERA *turn their chairs around to face the audience. They kneel on the chairs and sing.*

MRS. DOMÍNGUEZ:	MRS. CABRERA:
Virgen del Carmen . . .	Virgen del Cobre . . .

They stop at the same time, look at each other.

MRS. CABRERA: Excúsame, Gloria, but la Virgen del Carmen is a Puerto Rican virgin. I'm the one with the problem, chica. Don't you think we should pray to a Cuban virgin?

MRS. DOMÍNGUEZ: Excuse me, Sylvia, but I am the one handling this. You are not even a Catholic!

MRS. CABRERA: When you are in trouble you have to be ecumenical.

MRS. DOMÍNGUEZ: Okay. Then let's pray to both. Por si acaso.

MRS. DOMÍNGUEZ *and* MRS. CABRERA *sing.*

"SONG TO LA VIRGEN"
(Guaguancó)

MRS. CABRERA:	MRS. DOMÍNGUEZ:
VIRGEN DEL COBRE	
	VIRGEN DEL CARMEN
AYÚDANOS HOY	
	HELP US THIS DAY
DANOS UN TECHO	
	GIVE US A ROOF
PARA VIVIR	

MI VIRGENCITA

A PLACE TO LIVE

Y TODOS LOS SANTOS

OH HOLY VIRGIN

YO TE LO RUEGO

AND ALL THE SPIRITS

HAZME UN FAVOR

DO ME A FAVOR

I BEG OF YOU

MI VIRGENCITA

OH HOLY VIRGIN

RUEGA POR MÍ

PLEASE PRAY FOR ME

PLEASE PRAY FOR US

RUEGA POR MÍ

VIRGEN DEL COBRE

VIRGEN DEL CARMEN

VIRGEN DEL CARMEN

VIRGEN DEL COBRE

AYÚDANOS HOY

HELP US THIS DAY

MI VIRGENCITA

OH HOLY VIRGIN

HELP US THIS DAY

AYÚDANOS HOY

Black out. End of Act One.

ACT TWO

As the audience returns to their seats, part of the Overture will be played by LEILA. *Characters will be coming in one by one or in twos. Music continues playing as lights go down. In the dark we hear intro to the next song. As lights go up the characters are sitting in the same places they were in at the opening of the first act. There are more dummies now.* LEROY *is nervous and now and then looks into his shopping bag, as if to make sure something is indeed in there.* MOFETTI *enters from his office. He pauses in front of the door, breathes deeply, adjusts his tie, passes both his hands over the sides of his head and walks towards center stage.* MOFETTI *and the company sing.*

"GOOD AFTERNOON"

MOFETTI:
GOOD AFTERNOON
LADIES AND GENTLEMEN
GOOD AFTERNOON

CHORUS:
GOOD AFTERNOON
MR. MOFETTI:
GOOD AFTERNOON

MAILMAN:
GOOD AFTERNOON
MR. MOFETTI:
GOOD AFTERNOON

MOFETTI:
GOOD AFTERNOON
MR. POSTMAN
GOOD AFTERNOON

TELLERS:
GOOD AFTERNOON
MR. MOFETTI:

MOFETTI:
GOOD AFTERNOON
MY DEAR TELLERS
GOOD AFTERNOON

MOFETTI:
GOOD AFTERNOON
MY LOVELY LEILA:
GOOD AFTERNOON

LEILA:
GOOD AFTERNOON
MARCELLO (*Spoken.*) GET ON WITH IT

LEILA *abruptly stops playing.* MOFETTI *addresses the group in pompous oratory.*

MOFETTI: My dear, dear customers. My most appreciated colleagues ... today ... today is a special day. Since this bank was established at the turn of the century in this very neighborhood, it has been more than just a bank. I feel it is indeed appropriate that I speak to you at this moment, during one of our concerts, because I think that these events are perhaps the most important characteristic of this bank. We are one of the very few banking institutions in the city still providing this service to the customers ... . These concerts have taken place through two world wars, through the Depression, when the neighborhood changed, when the customers changed, through bad times, through good times ... And today, it is my duty to ... today, I have to inform you that ... today's concert marks ... a special ocassion ... a very special ocassion ... today ... today is ... LEILA'S BIRTHDAY!

LEILA: (*Standing up.* LEROY *jumps up from his seat.*) MY birthday? Marcello ...

LEROY: HER birthday!

MOFETTI: (*To* LEILA, *apologetic.*) I couldn't do it! (*To everybody, exiting to his office.*) I ... I'll get the ... champagne! (MOFETTI *runs to his office.* LEILA *tries to stop him. Everybody applauds.* LEILA *is surrounded by well-wishers.*)

MRS. DOMÍNGUEZ: I won't ask how many!

MRS. BORESTEIN: I wish I had known before ...

FRED: Many happy returns!

TELLERS: Happy birthday, Mrs. Zukov!

MAILMAN: Enjoy your day.

LEILA: Thank you, thank you, but ...

TELLER 2: Let's celebrate!

TELLER 1: Like in the old times!

MRS. BORESTEIN: Leila, sing us one of your old favorites.

MRS. DOMÍNGUEZ: Yes, yes. Remember when you used to say that you wanted to be the first female Liberace? (*Everybody laughs.*)

LEILA: But really, it is not ...

MAILMAN: Come on, Miss Zukov. It is a special day.

LEROY: (*Mysterious.*) It sure is.

LEILA: But ...

MRS. BORESTEIN: Why don't you play Mrs. Cabrera's favorite ... what's the name of that waltz she used to play in Havana?

MRS. DOMÍNGUEZ: It was "Over the Waves," but Sylvia is not here today. So we don't have to listen to that again.

TELLER 2: Yes, play something else.
TELLER 1: Yes, play YOUR favorite.
LEILA: That song is not what it used to be. (LEILA *sits at the piano. She plays and sings.*)

"LEILA'S THEME" (Reprise)

LIFE IS A BOWL OF CHERRIES
LIFE IS A CABARET
UNDER THE FULL MOON
ROWING ON THE LAKE
HAPPY SHOOTING THE BREEZE

LIFE IS A BOWL OF CHERRIES
LIFE IS A CABARET
UNDER THE FULL MOON
ROWING ON THE LAKE
HAPPY SHOOTING THE BREEZE
HAPPY SHOOTING THE BREEZE
HAPPY SHOOTING THE BREEZE

Everyone applauds.

MRS. BORESTEIN: Ah, that was lovely! We always have such good times . . .
MAILMAN: We sure do, Mrs. Borestein. I'm gonna miss this place . . . and all of you.
MRS. BORESTEIN: Are you leaving?
MRS. DOMÍNGUEZ: Did you win big at the horses?
LEILA: Oh, Eddie . . . It is about that letter you wrote, isn't it?
MAILMAN: Yes, Miss Zukov. I delivered a letter to myself this morning. From the Postmaster General himself. I've been transferred. To the South Bronx.
FRED: Poor man. Hardship duty.
MAILMAN: It won't be harder than this neighborhood at one time. I used to be threatened to death for not delivering welfare checks on time. Not anymore, though. I hardly know the people I deliver mail to. You are the only people I know. Everybody else has moved. I don't really want to go, but I've got my orders.
LEROY: Did they give you a reason for the transfer?
MAILMAN: No.
LEROY: Maybe it's your looks, Eddie. Maybe they're getting "designer mailmen"—to go with the rest of the neighborhood, you know.

LEILA: I'm so sorry, Eddie. We'll miss you.

MRS. DOMÍNGUEZ: We have to give you a farewell party.

FRED: Here?

MRS. BORESTEIN: Sure. We have celebrated many occasions here.

MRS. DOMÍNGUEZ: When Sylvia's son, Enrique, graduated from City College, Mr. Mofetti threw a party for him, right here in the bank. He did the same for Tina Wong.

FRED: Who's that?

MRS. DOMÍNGUEZ: The daughter of Mr. Wong, of Wong's Chinese Laundry. That was before your time. She had just passed the bar exam. That was a big party! Imagine, she was the first lawyer born and bred in the neighborhood. Mr. Wong was so happy he did everybody's laundry free for a month! (*Everybody laughs.*)

LEILA: A very bright young lady. (*Looking at* MOFETTI.) And courageous.

MRS. BORESTEIN: And when Leroy was in the hospital for a long time after coming back from the war, we used to tape Leila's concerts and send him the cassettes to the hospital.

LEROY: I sure appreciated that. It made me come back to the neighborhood. I felt I had friends here. But I had had other plans. I made all kinds of mental plans in that hospital bed.

LEILA: Yes, we are friends here. We've had good times and bad times, as Marce ... Mr. Mofetti said.

LEROY: (*Glaring at* FRED, *then at the dummies.*) Too bad outsiders and newcomers can't appreciate that.

FRED: You are wrong about me. I am not an outsider. I was born here, in this neighborhood. Two blocks away, as a matter of fact. (*Everyone is surprised by the news.*)

MRS. DOMÍNGUEZ: You're putting us on. How come you never told us before?

LEROY: I don't believe it.

MRS. BORESTEIN: Funny, I don't remember you ... but then, there are so many things I don't remember.

FRED: Oh yes, my mother lived in that house—the one that now has the expensive Central American arts and crafts—for many years. When the neighborhood went bad ...

MRS. DOMÍNGUEZ: (*To* MRS. BORESTEIN.) He means when I opened my botánica.

FRED: ... she decided she didn't want to raise her children here. She dreamed of the suburbs. Meaning Queens. So we moved there. I went to Catholic school in Elmhurst. Then that neighborhood began to change too. We moved to a small town in New Jersey. That changed too. We ended up in Connecticut ... But I always liked this neighborhood, so when I read that this was going to be the next Soho, I bought an old house ... I got it real cheap. It is an investment that's paying up ... also, I feel I am helping improve the neighborhood by moving back here.

LEROY: (*To himself.*) Asshole.

MRS. BORESTEIN: Your mother must be very proud of you.

FRED: I'm not so sure. She can't understand why, after she worked so hard to get me out of this neighborhood, I've come back. (*Sings.*)

"GENTRIFICATION"

I TELL MY MAMÁ WHAT'S HAPPENING IN THE NEIGHBORHOOD
BUT SHE DOESN'T GET IT, CAN'T UNDERSTAND WHAT'S GOING ON
I EXPLAIN TO HER THAT EL VIEJO BARRIO IS NOT THE SAME
THINGS ARE CHANGING, THEY ARE CHANGING
NOW WE'RE PLAYING A BRAND NEW GAME

YOU BUY A HOUSE, THEN YOU FIX IT UP, YOU'LL MAKE TWICE AS MUCH
TO OWN A CONDO IS THE NEW FRONTIER, THE NEW GOLD RUSH
THERE'S THE NEW BOUTIQUE, THE CROISSANTERIE AND THE ARTS AND CRAFTS
THEN RENTS GO UP, THEY KEEP GOING UP
AND SOME PEOPLE GET THE SHAFT
BUT ALL SHE SAYS IS
OYE M'IJITO, EXPLAIN AGAIN
QUÉ ES LO QUE PASA
WHAT'S GOING ON
OYE, M'IJITO, EXPLAIN AGAIN
NO ENTIENDO NADA
EXPLÍCAMELO BIEN

I TELL MY MAMÁ, IT'S VERY SIMPLE TO UN-

DERSTAND
THIS LITTLE ISLAND IS TURNING INTO A WONDERLAND
IT'S MY MANHATTAN, I WANNA PIECE OF THAT APPLE PIE
YOU'LL BE PROUD OF ME, I'LL BE PROUD OF ME
WHEN I'M RICH WAY BEFORE YOU DIE

I EXPLAIN TO HER THAT THE NEW IDEAL IS TO MAKE A BUCK
TO WEAR THE LATEST, TO EAT THE BEST TO OWN SOME STOCK
THE GREATEST THING THAT HAS EVER HAPPENED IN GENERATIONS
THE OLD TURF, THIS OLD TURF
IS GOING THROUGH GENTRIFICATION

BUT ALL SHE SAYS IS
GENTRIFICATION, QUÉ COSA ES ESO
OYE, M'IJITO, EXPLAIN AGAIN
WHATEVER HAPPENED A TOA LA GENTE
THAT LIVED IN THE BARRIO
FROM LONG AGO

GENTRIFICATION, MAMÁ
GENTRIFICACIÓN
NO ENTIENDO NADA
SHE SAYS TO ME
GENTRIFICATION, MAMÁ
GENTRIFICACIÓN
LOS TIEMPOS CAMBIAN
AND WE MOVE AHEAD
GENTRIFICATION, MAMÁ
GENTRIFICACIÓN

Everybody joins in the chorus, each one giving a different meaning to the word "gentrification." MRS. CABRERA *enters from the street. She's crying loudly. Music stops.*

LEILA: Mrs. Cabrera!
MRS. DOMÍNGUEZ: Sylvia, what's the matter?
MRS. CABRERA: Ay, chica, that brujería you gave me didn't work! All the opposite.

FRED: Witchcraft? What is she talking about?

MRS. CABRERA: The landlord was going to raise my husband's rent at the restaurant 300 percent. And Gloria here gave me some leaves to put in the envelope with the rent check to make him change his mind. But it didn't work. (*She cries.*) Now he will raise the rent 400 percent!

MRS. BORESTEIN: Gotten Nyu!

MAILMAN: Ay, bendito!

MRS. DOMÍNGUEZ: Well, like I said, sometimes it works, sometimes it doesn't.

MRS. CABRERA: Jacinto is desperate. He says he's closing down the restaurant and going down to Miami. I know he won't be happy there. He can't retire yet. He's a workaholic. He will die before his time!

MRS. DOMÍNGUEZ: Nah. I thought the same thing would happen to me when I had to close my botánica. And see, here I am. I keep myself busy doing part-time trabajitos.

MRS. BORESTEIN: It is terrible what's happening. This ... this ... purification ...

FRED: Gentrification.

MRS. BORESTEIN: That. Do you know that Leroy has also lost his apartment?

LEROY: Mrs. B., please ...

LEILA: Leroy, why didn't you tell me?

FRED: Hey, man, I'm sorry to hear that. (LEROY *glares at* FRED.)

MRS. DOMÍNGUEZ: Oh poor Leroy! What are you going to do?

LEROY: I have plans.

MRS. BORESTEIN: I would ask him to move in with me, but you know, they don't allow men in there ... I mean young ones.

LEROY: Thank you, Mrs. B. Thank you.

MRS. CABRERA: I don't know where we can go. Rents are even worse in other parts of the city.

FRED: There's always the river. Boat houses, like in Hong Kong. They could make Manhattan quite exotic ... Think of it—rice and beans on the East River ...

LEROY: (LEROY *gets up and goes for* FRED'*s throat.* MRS. CABRERA *and* MRS. DOMÍNGUEZ *hold* LEROY *back. The* MAILMAN *stands in front of* FRED.) I'll kill him! I'll kill him!

FRED: But what have I done to him?

MAILMAN: Hablas mucha mierda, mi pana!

MOFETTI: (MOFETTI *enters from his office with a tray loaded with champagne glasses.*) Here's the champagne! (MOFETTI *puts the tray with champagne glasses on top of the piano. Everyone helps himself.*)

MRS. CABRERA: Champagne for what?

MRS. BORESTEIN: It's Leila's birthday! How wonderful! I love champagne. I haven't had a glass since my last trip to Atlantic City . . . and that must have been back in nineteen . . .

MAILMAN: (MOFETTI *offers a glass to* LEILA, *who's fuming.*) I propose a toast to Leila. (*Everyone lifts the glasses and freezes. Spot on the piano.* MOFETTI *has also raised his glass.* LEILA *plays.* MOFETTI *sings.*)

"LEILA AT NOONTIME"

LEILA AT NOONTIME
IVORY MELTS UNDER YOUR HANDS
MELODY DRIPS FROM YOUR FINGERS
YOUR FACE AND YOUR EYES ARE AGLOW
BRIGHT STARS ON THE PIANO BLACK TOP

LEILA AT MIDDAY
TIME SEEMS TO BE AT A STANDSTILL
THE SUN BENDS AND LISTENS TO YOU
THE DAYS ARE LONG AND BRIGHTER
REGARDLESS OF WINTER OR FALL

LEILA AT NIGHTTIME
I SLEEP IN A HAMMOCK
OF MUSICAL DREAMS
I HOLD YOUR HAND IN MINE
AND THE MUSIC BELONGS TO ME
I AM BACH, CHOPIN
BEETHOVEN AND BRAHMS
JUST FROM TOUCHING YOUR HAND
JUST FROM TOUCHING YOUR HAND

After the song, full lights come up on the whole scene. Everyone is still holding the glasses up high. Immediately VICTORIA FRIBBLE *and her assistant enter.* VICTORIA *has red hair, wears large dark glasses and is dressed in black-and red-striped leotards and black leg warmers.*

VICTORIA: (*To* MOFETTI.) Ah, Mr. Mofetti! I see you were expecting me. How kind of you. This is quite a welcome! Thank you very much. (VICTORIA *takes the glass of champagne from* MOFETTI'*s hand. Her assistant takes a glass away from someone else. They look around the bank.*)

MOFETTI: (*To* LEILA.) Who is she?

LEILA: That's Victoria Fribble!

MOFETTI: Victoria Fribble! ... Ah, yes, Ms. Fribble, of course ... why don't you ... er ... come into my office to discuss your ... er ... new account.

LEILA: (*Exasperated. Whispering.*) There you go again! This is a perfect moment to tell them!

MOFETTI: (*Whispering.*) Let me handle this.

VICTORIA: I came to check out the place. This is my assistant, Jane.

JANE: Hi!

MOFETTI: Hi.

VICTORIA: (*Looking around.*) Not bad ... not bad at all. Of course it needs some changes ... (*Bends down to touch the floor.*) ... Maybe a new floor ... Hmmm ... I don't know ... Jane, let's try it. (*The two lie on the floor and begin to do exercises a la Jane Fonda. They sing along.*)

"AEROBICS"

LEFT RIGHT
RIGHT LEFT
STRETCH
STRETCH
BREATH
BREATH

AND GRIND
SLIM YOUR WAIST
FLATTEN YOUR TUMMY
HARDEN YOUR ASS
DON'T BE A FAT DUMMY

LEROY: (*Before the number is over,* LEROY *pulls down a ski mask over his face, pulls out a gun from the shopping bag and points it at* VICTORIA *and* JANE.) HOLD IT EVERYBODY, STOP THIS SHIT! Nobody moves. This is a hold up! (*To women.*) You two, in there! You are my hostages. (*Everybody screams. Women go into* TELLERS' *cages.* LEROY *gives them the shopping bag.*) Here, take this. Fill it with money. Big bills. Nothing smaller than fives. And if any of you touches that alarm button, I start shooting!

VICTORIA: (*Hysterical.*) I don't even know where it is!

MRS. BORESTEIN: Leroy, what do you think you're doing?

LEROY: I'm robbing this bank, Mrs.B! That's what I'm doing! Robbing this bank!

MRS. DOMÍNGUEZ: But it is our money!

LEROY: Not any more!

MOFETTI: (LEILA *pushes* MOFETTI *forward, urging him to do something.*) Mr. Young, if I may have a word with you . . .

LEROY: Don't Mister Young me, Marcello!

LEILA: Leroy, this is crazy!

FRED: Somebody should call the police!

MOFETTI: Nobody calls anybody. We'll take care of this ourselves. We are all friends here. Leroy . . .

LEROY: Shut up, Mofetti! You ain't no friend of mine. You are chicken. I have no chicken friends. When I needed you, you didn't come through!

MRS. DOMÍNGUEZ: Come through? With what? What?

MRS. CABRERA: What's going on here?

MOFETTI: Leroy, put that gun away and come here. Let's discuss this in a logical manner. I know you are upset about losing your apartment . . .

FRED: I wish I had my computer with me right now.

MRS. BORESTEIN: We'll help you find an apartment.

LEILA: We won't call the police.

MRS. CABRERA: Maybe my husband can get you a job in the restaurant.

MOFETTI: Leroy, I'll give you one more chance . . . (*Music begins.*)

LEROY: Sure! Tell me more! You keep us entertained with your concerts and sing-alongs while you keep OUR money, but when we need a loan to move or to buy a house, we can't get it!

MOFETTI: I don't make the rules and regulations . . . believe me, Leroy . . .

LEROY: I asked you for a loan to move and you denied it to me . . . I had no collateral! (*Sings.*)

"MAKE ME BELIEVE"

I HAVE TO BELIEVE
I HAVE A CHANCE
I HAVE TO BELIEVE
MY HANDS WILL COME OUT CLEAN
AFTER HANDLING THE DIRT
I HAVE TO BELIEVE
MY MOUTH WON'T BLEED
AFTER CHEWING THE GLASS

MAKE ME BELIEVE THAT
I HAVE THAT CHANCE
MAKE ME BELIEVE
AND I'LL RUN

I HAVE TO BELIEVE
I HAVE A CHANCE
I HAVE TO BELIEVE
I'LL STILL ENJOY THE FLOWERS
WHEN THE FOUL AIR CLEARS
I HAVE TO BELIEVE
I'LL SEE THE LIGHT
AFTER DARKNESS HAS PASSED

MAKE ME BELIEVE THAT
I HAVE THAT CHANCE
MAKE ME BELIEVE
AND I'LL RUN
I CAN WIN THE PRIZE
AT THE END OF THE RACE
IF YOU MAKE ME BELIEVE

I BELIEVE
I HAVE TO BELIEVE
DEEP INSIDE
I'LL HAVE A CHANCE AT PEACE
I'LL GET A CRACK AT LOVE
I HAVE TO BELIEVE
I HAVE TO BELIEVE

MAKE ME BELIEVE THAT
I HAVE THAT CHANCE

MAKE ME BELIEVE
AND I'LL RUN
I CAN WIN THE PRICE
AT THE END OF THE RACE
IF YOU MAKE ME BELIEVE
IF YOU MAKE ME BELIEVE

MOFETTI: Leroy, please ... let me explain ...

LEROY: Explain! I don't believe a word you'd say Mofetti! You are a liar. Why don't you tell them! Tell them the truth! Tell them the bank is closing! Tell them it is going to be a Victoria Fribble Body Shop!

VICTORIA: (*Sticking her head out of a* TELLER'*s window.*) That's me!

LEROY: Get back in there!

MRS. CABRERA: Is this true, Mr. Mofetti?

LEILA: (*To* MOFETTI.) I told you!

MRS. DOMÍNGUEZ: Come on, Mr. Mofetti, out with it!

MOFETTI: It is true ... all of it.

LEILA: You forgot the condos.

MOFETTI: Yes. The apartments upstairs will be turned into luxury condominiums.

LEILA: So, dear friends, today is not my birthday. Today is really my last concert.

MRS. BORESTEIN: (*Very agitated.*) I can't believe it! I can't believe it! (*Everyone turns towards* MRS. BORESTEIN.)

MRS. DOMÍNGUEZ: What? What is it?

MRS. BORESTEIN: I remember everything! I remember the plots of all my novels! All of them! Even the ones I never wrote! I remember it all! Oh God ... I remember ... Atlantic City is full of gambling parlors! (MRS. BORESTEIN *collapses on a chair. Everyone runs towards her.* FRED *takes her pulse.* LEROY *runs to* MRS. BORESTEIN. *In the commotion* VICTORIA FRIBBLE *and her assistant escape.*)

FRED: I think she's dead. I can't feel her pulse.

LEROY: (LEROY *pushes* FRED *aside. Kneels down next to* MRS. BORESTEIN *and puts his ear to her heart.*) Don't die, old mamma! Not now. I was robbing this bank for you. To go to Atlantic City, to walk down the boardwalk, under your parasol.

FRED: You did it for her! Well, see what you've done! You've killed her! (LEROY *gets up and punches* FRED *who falls flat on the floor.* MRS. DOMÍNGUEZ *holds back* LEROY.)

MRS. DOMÍNGUEZ: Leroy, haven't you caused enough trouble? ... Poor MRS. Borestein. She was such a lovely lady.

MRS. CABRERA: Una dama. Una verdadera dama.

MOFETTI: I'll call an ambulance. (*Exits to his office.*)

MAILMAN: This is all so terrible. I don't know what to say.

LEILA *goes to the piano and begins to play a mournful melody.* MOFETTI *returns. Front drop comes down. Now we see the action from outside.* LEILA *sings, the others join in one by one.*

"ONE LAST SONG"

CLOSE THE PIANO LID
PUT AWAY THE MUSIC SHEET
TURN OFF THE LOBBY LIGHTS
THIS CONCERT IS OUR LAST

ONE LAST SONG JUST TO SAY GOODBYE
ONE LAST SONG FOR THE TIMES WE HAD
WE WON'T SING TOGETHER AGAIN
OUR TIME IS UP, THE ENDING IS SAD

ONE LAST SONG FOR THE SAKE OF LOVE
ONE LAST SONG JUST BECAUSE WE CARE
WE WON'T SING TOGETHER AGAIN
OUR JOY IS GONE, VANISHED IN THE AIR

WE SANG OF OUR PLEASURE
WE SANG OF OUR PAIN
LIFE WAS SO EASY
SHARING IT WITH YOU
YOUR FEELINGS WERE MINE
AND MY MEMORY YOUR OWN
YOUR MUSIC'S MY MUSIC
MY SONG WAS YOUR SONG
IN THIS LAST CONCERT
I WANTED YOU TO KNOW

ONE LAST SONG JUST TO SAY GOODBYE
ONE LAST SONG FOR THE TIMES WE HAD

After the song there's a long pause. A PARAMEDIC *enters with a gurney.*

PARAMEDIC: Anybody called for an ambulance?

FRED: It's MRS. Borestein there.

PARAMEDIC: (*To* FRED *and* MAILMAN.) Put her on the stretcher, please. (*To* MRS. BORESTEIN *while she's being moved to gurney.*) Your name, please. Address? Age? Social Security number? Medicare? Blue Cross? Blue Shield? . . .

MRS. CABRERA: Can't you see she's dead!

PARAMEDIC: (*Taking* MRS. BORESTEIN'*s pulse.*) No, she ain't. She just passed out.

MAILMAN: Thank God for that! (*Simultaneous exclamations of relief from the others.*)

MRS. DOMÍNGUEZ: I knew the Virgin wouldn't let me down! (*A loud gong is heard. Lights go up on the audience. Everyone looks out the window.*) Ms. Wong!

FRED: Who? Where?

MRS. CABRERA: The attorney. Mr. Wong's daughter.

MRS. DOMÍNGUEZ: (*To* FRED.) I told you about her, remember?

LEILA: Oh, I'm so glad she came!

LEILA *plays reprise of "Song to la Virgen". Front drop flies up. Actors change set. Now we are inside the bank again. While this is happening,* MS. WONG *comes down the isle towards the stage. When she gets to the stage, the loud gong is heard again. Music stops.*

MS. WONG: Good afternoon.

ALL: Good afternoon.

MS. WONG: I have important news. With your permission, I'd like to share it with you. There's no time to waste. I am the new executive director of the Neighborhood Tenant's Association. The tenants have decided to fight to save our neighborhood. And we need your help.

LEILA: What can we do?

MS. WONG: We'll sue!

FRED: I don't think you have a chance.

MS. WONG: It is a better chance than sitting here, complaining about the situation. (*Murmurs of reaction.*)

MRS. CABRERA: How about my husband's rent increase?

MS. WONG: We'll sue!

LEROY: How about my apartment?

MS. WONG: We'll march!

MAILMAN: How about my transfer?

MS. WONG: We'll lobby!

MOFETTI: How about the bank?
MS. WONG: We'll picket! But we won't be moved!
LEILA: (*Holding on to* MOFFETTI'*s arm.*) How about us?
MS. WONG: I'll get you a divorce!
FRED: That all sounds very easy, but how about the laws?
MS. WONG: We'll change them! ... That's why I'm also running for the City Council. As you know, Chinatown has been pushed so far this way that now we are in the same district. I need your vote. Each one of you can make a difference if you vote!
FRED: But you can't stop progress! I mean, after you have the computer, you can't go back to the abacus. (*To all.*) Don't you want things to change?
MRS. CABRERA: Of course, we do. But we want to be part of the change.
LEROY: That's right. We don't want to be pushed around.
FRED: But you didn't do anything when the junkies took over the place.
LEROY: Yeah, we didn't. Maybe we've learned a lesson. Maybe now we can do something about the yuppies taking over the place.
MRS. CABRERA: And the real estate sharks.
MRS. DOMÍNGUEZ: But what can we do? It's too late. It's too late for me. It is much too late for MRS. Borestein ...
PARAMEDIC: It is too late for me. The hospital is closing down too! (*The* PARAMEDIC *begins to push* MRS. BORESTEIN *towards the street door.* MRS. BORESTEIN *begins to revive.*)
MS. WONG: It is not too late if you get involved, get yourselves organized. Then, we can sue, we can march, we can picket! But it will be too late if you just sit here singing old songs while the neighborhood disappears right in front of your eyes! Life is not a bowl of cherries, you know!
PARAMEDIC: I don't think any of that will really help.
MRS. BORESTEIN: (*From gurney, weakly.*) Yes, yes! We'll sue! (*Everyone rejoices at* MRS. BORESTEIN'*s recuperation. The following lines are said almost simultaneously.*)
LEILA: MRS. Borestein!
MRS. DOMÍNGUEZ: She's really alive!
MRS. CABRERA: ¡Qué alegría!
PARAMEDIC: I knew I was good, but not that good!
MRS. BORESTEIN: We'll march!
ALL (*except* FRED.): We'll march!

MRS. BORESTEIN: We'll picket!

ALL (*Except* FRED.): We'll picket!

MRS. BORESTEIN: But we won't be moved!

ALL (*Except* FRED.): But we won't be moved! (FRED *is to one side, away from the action. He feels isolated. He clears his throat. Everyone turns towards him, waiting.* FRED *clears his throat again.*)

MRS. CABRERA: Fred, I was thinking ... maybe you can help too ...

FRED: Me?

LEROY: That'll be the day.

MAILMAN: Yeah, man. With your computer!

LEILA: That's a wonderful idea!

FRED: (*Halfheartedly.*) Nah, nah.

MOFETTI: Fred, we need you on our side.

FRED: Well, I don't know ... that would require designing a special program. I don't know if I can do it.

MRS. CABRERA: I'm sure you can do it.

ALL (*Except* MRS. BORESTEIN.): Come on, Fred! Sure, you can do it! You are a wiz! (etc.)

FRED: Maybe.

LEROY: And while you are at it, why don't you also program your heart and rent one of your apartments to MRS. Domínguez?

MRS. DOMÍNGUEZ: Oh yes, I'd love to move back here!

FRED: And have a botánica in MY building? Oh, no!

MRS. DOMÍNGUEZ: We could negotiate that.

FRED: I'll think about it.

MRS. BORESTEIN: (*Getting up from the gurney.*) How about Atlantic City? (*Music begins.*)

MRS. BORESTEIN: We'll march! We'll picket! We'll sue!

ALL: But we won't be moved! (*They sing.*)

"WE WON'T BE MOVED"

WHEN THE BARRIO WENT UP IN FLAMES
WHEN THE CITY WAS DEEP IN TROUBLE
THEY SHOOK THEIR HEADS "OH WHAT A SHAME"
AND WENT RUNNING TO THE SUBURBS

NOW THE CHILDREN ARE COMING BACK
LIKE AN INVASION OF HOME SNATCHERS
AND THE PEOPLE THAT STAYED BEHIND

FIND NO PLACE TO HANG THEIR HATS
BUT WE WON'T BE MOVED
WE WON'T BE MOVED
WE'RE STAYING HERE
WE'RE STAYING PUT
WE WON'T BE MOVED
WE WON'T BE MOVED
GOING NOWHERE
WE'RE HOLDING ON
'CAUSE WE BELONG

NOW THE CITY'S A BIG BOUTIQUE
AND WE ARE LIKE WINDOW SHOPPERS
NOSES PRESSING ON THE GLASS TO PEEK
AT THE GOODIES WE CAN'T AFFORD

NO CITY CAN BE AN ISLAND
JUST A PIECE OF REAL ESTATE
IT NEEDS A SOUL, IT'S GOT TO SMILE
ON ALL ITS PEOPLE TO BE GREAT
BUT WE WON'T BE MOVED
WE WON'T BE MOVED
WE'RE STAYING HERE
WE'RE STAYING PUT
WE WON'T BE MOVED
OUT TO THE RIVER
WE WON'T BE MOVED
UP TO THE BRONX
WE WON'T BE MOVED
WE'RE STAYING HERE
WE'RE GONNA SUE
OUR HOMES ARE HERE
AND WE WON'T BE MOVED!

During the song everyone will participate in a choreography in which the chairs will again be rolled around the stage, and the dummies moved from chair to chair and some of them placed elsewhere on the stage. Extra chairs may be brought in so that there's room for everyone. With the last lines, the company will move its chairs downstage, facing the audience, and sit on them with determination, crossing arms across chests.

Black out.

The End

PANTALLAS

Comedia apocalíptica en un acto

1986

Pantallas

PERSONAJES

ELENA: Actriz de telenovelas. Cuarentona. Bella, pero algo ajada. Resignada. Vive de sus recuerdos, se aferra a su fama de ayer.

ROBERTO: Actor de telenovelas. De 22 años de edad. Joven y bello, lleno de ilusiones sobre el futuro de su carrera artística.

ESCENOGRAFÍA

La sala de una casa de playa en un país del Caribe. Amueblada modestamente con una mezcla de estilos tropicales, pero con buen gusto. En el foro derecho, un sofá y una mesa baja al frente domina la habitación. Al lado, otra mesita más alta con un teléfono. A la izquierda del escenario, un bar con dos banquetas altas, vasos, botellas de bebida y un pequeño televisor. Al fondo y al centro, una ventana grande con persianas. Dos sillas de espaldar alto están colocadas a ambos lados de la ventana. A la izquierda, detrás del bar, una puerta que da a otra habitación de la casa.

TIEMPO DE LA ACCIÓN

Toda la obra ocurre en un día en el futuro cercano. Tal vez mañana mismo. Ojalá nunca.

Pantallas was first performed at Duo Theater in New York City, on April 17, 1986 with the following cast:

ELENA .... Susana Tubert
ROBERTO .... Arcadio Ruiz
MAURICIO .... Jorge Luis Ramos

It was directed by Arcadio Ruiz. *Pantallas* is included in *Cuban Theater in the United States: A Critical Anthology*, edited and translated by Luis González Cruz and Francesca Colecchia, published by Bilingual Review Press.

PRIMER ACTO

Al encenderse las luces ELENA *y* MAURICIO *están sentados en el sofá, besándose apasionadamente. La puerta se abre súbitamente y entra* ROBERTO.

ROBERTO: ¡Así quería encontrarlos! Ya me lo sospechaba. Sí, lo he sospechado desde hace mucho tiempo. Era un presentimiento, algo que me roía las entrañas, que me quitaba el sueño. (*Saca una pistola.*) Pero al fin todo ha terminado. ¡Esta noche dormiré en paz! (*Les apunta, pero la mano comienza a temblarle. Baja la pistola, se lleva la mano a la cabeza. Habla a sí mismo.*) ¿Qué hago? Esto es una ridiculez. ¡Un marido moderno no actuaría así! (*A* MAURICIO *y* ELENA.) Olvídense. Sigan. (ROBERTO *sale.* ELENA *y* MAURICIO, *que habían estado petrificados del miedo dan un suspiro de alivio, se miran, sonríen y comienzan a besarse de nuevo. La puerta se abre, entra* ROBERTO. *Contempla la escena algo sorprendido, sin alterarse se recupera, sonríe, se suelta la corbata.*) Ah, querida . . . Mauricio . . . ¿cómo están? Día caluroso, no? (*Va hacia el bar y sirve unos tragos. Los trae al sofá. Se sienta al otro lado de* ELENA, *quien ahora queda entre los dos hombres.*)

ELENA: (*Turbada.*) Roberto, mi amor, no sabía que llegarías temprano hoy. Pensé que . . .

ROBERTO: Perdona que no te avisara que regresaría temprano. Perdona la inconveniencia, mi vida. (*Dándole en la rodilla a* MAURICIO.) Y tú, Mauricio, mi viejo amigo, ¿cómo te va?

MAURICIO: (*Turbado.*) Bien, muy bien. Le contaba a Elena que . . .

ROBERTO: Déjense de hacerse los tontos. Yo sé muy bien lo que estaban haciendo. No soy un estúpido. Miren, ya hace tiempo que me olía esto. Me daba vueltas en la cabeza constantemente, como un dolor de muelas.

ELENA: ¡Ay Roberto, mi vida, perdóname! Esta es la primera vez. Tú lo sabes muy bien. ¡En doce años de casados yo jamás te he sido infiel!

MAURICIO: Ha sido algo súbito, inesperado, una locura . . .

ROBERTO: (*Calmadamente se pone de pie.*) ¿Saben que los voy a matar a los dos, verdad? Tengo que hacerlo, en defensa de mi honor. (*Saca la pistola.*)

ELENA: (*Tirándose de rodillas al piso y gritando melodramáticamente.*) ¡No, mi amor, no, no lo hagas! ¡Piensa en nuestros hijos!

ROBERTO: (*Confundido.*) Pero, si no tenemos hijos ...

ELENA: ¡Lo sé, pero si me matas nunca los tendremos!

MAURICIO: (*Poniéndose de pie, saliéndose de situación.*) Ay, a mí esto no me gusta nada.

ELENA: A mí tampoco.

ROBERTO: Sí, tienen razón. Esto está algo trillado.

MAURICIO: La idea del triángulo amoroso, la infidelidad, todo eso está bien. Eso siempre gusta. El engaño atrae a todo el mundo ... Pero, no sé ... creo que podríamos ser más originales.

ROBERTO: Sí, no debía sacar la pistola en ese momento.

ELENA: No sólo eso, no me puedes matar a mí así, tan pronto. Quedamos en que los tres papeles principales serían igualmente importantes y que nadie desaparecería hasta el último capítulo.

ROBERTO: Sí, ese fue el acuerdo. Esto fue solo una idea.

ELENA: Bueno, pues esa idea no resultó.

ROBERTO: Vamos a probar otra cosa.

MAURICIO: Yo no sé si éste es un buen método. Tal vez debíamos discutir la idea antes, pensar un poco la situación antes de ...

ELENA: Estoy de acuerdo. Debemos ser un poco más científicos —analizar los temas, los personajes, tiempo, lugar, espacio— antes de lanzarnos a improvisar escenas.

ROBERTO: (*A* ELENA.) Eso me parece innecesario. Hemos actuado en decenas de telenovelas. ¿No crees que a estas alturas ya sabemos lo que funciona o no?

MAURICIO: Ustedes me perdonan, pero con todo respeto a la experiencia de ustedes dos, a mí me parece que sería más apropiado conseguir un escritor para que desarrolle el guión. Después de todo, nosotros sólo somos actores.

ROBERTO: Los escritores de verdad no quieren perder el tiempo haciendo telenovelas.

ELENA: Además, les pagan muy poco ...

ROBERTO: Y las quieren hacer muy serias, o intelectuales.

ELENA: En realidad, no necesitamos un escritor.

ROBERTO: Además, en estos momentos, ¿dónde lo vamos a encontrar?

ELENA: No se preocupen, tenemos muchísimo tiempo para desarrollar este guión.

MAURICIO: (*Cambiando el tema.*) Sí, tienen razón, es mejor escribirlo nosotros mismos. Así tenemos control absoluto de los papeles que vamos a hacer. Estaremos en todos los capítulos, cobraremos más . . .

ELENA: Nos haremos famosos de nuevo. Todo el mundo nos reconocerá en la calle, como antes. Nos pedirán autógrafos en el supermercado. Haremos especiales de televisión. Viajaremos por toda América Latina. Grabaremos discos con las estrellas del momento . . .

MAURICIO: Pero, si no somos cantantes.

ELENA: Eso no importa. Seremos famosos y la fama obra milagros en el talento de los que la obtienen. Yo me veo cantando en el Estadio Central, ante 30,000 espectadores. (*Canta.*)

"Algo de mí, algo de mí
algo de mí se va muriendo
quiero vivir, quiero vivir . . . "

MAURICIO: (*Entusiasmado.*) ¡Las muchachas se desmayarán cuando yo suba al escenario, se quitarán la ropa gritando mi nombre —Ma-u-ri-cio, Ma-u-ri-cio!

ROBERTO: Yo me conformo con recibir un cheque todas las semanas por hacer lo que me gusta: actuar.

ELENA: ¡Ay, tú nunca llegarás a nada! Piensas en pequeño, te conformas con lo cotidiano, lo común y corriente. En la vida hay que tener aspiraciones épicas, querido mío.

ROBERTO: Estamos perdiendo el tiempo con estas fantasías infantiles. Vamos a seguir, a ver, otra idea . . .

ELENA: Ideas . . . ideas, eso, ideas magistrales, ¿verdad? Siempre buscando ideas, ideas de otros. Eres como una sanguijuela de la mente. A ti nunca se te ocurre una idea propia. Ah, pero hay que reconocer que tienes una habilidad superior para utilizar las ideas de los demás, apropiarte de ellas y sacarles dinero. ¿Te das cuenta que has llegado a la posición que tienes gracias a ideas ajenas? ¿No te da vergüenza? ¿No te sientes . . . mínimo?

ROBERTO: En lo absoluto. Ese es mi negocio: las ideas. Sean de quien sean. Hay muchos que tienen ideas extraordinarias, pero no hacen nada con ellas. ¡Esos, que se vayan al diablo! Y tú, no te quejes tanto. Vives muy bien a costa de mis ideas "ajenas".

ELENA: Ja, ja, ja. Vivo bien, sí. Muy bien. Una mansión en la Colonia San Miguel, diez criadas, tres automóviles, mi peluquera particular, viajes a Europa, abrigos de visón. Sí, querido mío, vivo muy bien, pero lo único que tus ideas usurpadas no han logrado darme es ... la felicidad.

ROBERTO: Ahí está tu grave error, María Eugenia de la Campa: esperar que otros te den la felicidad. ¿Se te ha ocurrido alguna vez tratar de hacerte feliz a ti misma?

ELENA: Sí. Me he masturbado en numerosas ocasiones, pero ...

MAURICIO: ¡Corten! ¡Corten!

ROBERTO: Pero, ¿por qué, si íbamos tan bien?

ELENA: Estuve regia, ¿no?

MAURICIO: ¡Si serán lerdos! ¿Pero no se dan cuenta? ¡En televisión no se puede decir "masturbar"!

ELENA: ¿Quién dice?

MAURICIO: ¿Quién dice? ¿Tú has oído alguna vez a Johanna Rosaly decir "masturbar"? ¿Tú has oído alguna vez a Libertad Lamarque —La Novia de América— decir "masturbar"? ¿Tú has oído a Sully Díaz, a "Coralito", decir "masturbar"?

ELENA: (*Piensa.*) Bueno ... no, en televisión no.

ROBERTO: Bien, bien. No se puede utilizar lenguaje contemporáneo. Tenemos que ser más cuidadosos ... más clásicos.

MAURICIO: Clásicos. Hmmm. Hmmm. (*Da vuelta pensando.*) Eso. Clásicos. Con un clásico vamos a la segura.

ELENA: Ay, no. Para clásicos el teatro. La televisión debe ser moderna.

MAURICIO: No digo clásico clásico, sino una adaptación de un clásico. Trasponemos la acción al momento de hoy y ... ¡presto! Tenemos un hit.

ROBERTO: ¿Sí? ¿Cómo qué?

MAURICIO: Vamos a pensar. (*Piensa.*) Una historia universal, que tenga sentido y vigencia hoy en día. Algo así como ... ¡el *Don Juan Tenorio*!

ELENA: ¡Estás loco! Hoy en día con la liberación de la mujer, el *Don Juan* está desacreditado. Pasé.

ROBERTO: ¿Pasé? ¿Pero en qué mundo tú vives? Eso se da todos los días, m'ija, en todas partes del mundo. (*Con aire de conquistador.*) ¡Si lo sabré yo!

MAURICIO: (*Entusiasmado.*) Sí, sí. Vamos a experimentar con una escena. ¿Qué tal la de Don Luis y Don Juan en la posada?

ELENA: Un momento, un momento.

ROBERTO: ¿Qué pasa?

ELENA: Doña Inés no está en esa escena.

ROBERTO: ... Sí ... es verdad.

MAURICIO: Bueno, pues ... luego sale. En ésta puedes hacer de otra cosa.

ELENA: ¿Como qué?

MAURICIO: La mesera, por ejemplo.

ELENA: ¡Qué mesera, ni qué ocho cuartos! Yo quiero experimentar con Doña Inés ya mismo!

ROBERTO: (*Impaciente.*) Bueno, haz lo que quieras.

ELENA *se hace una cofia de monja poniéndose un paño blanco sobre la cabeza y se coloca detrás del bar.* MAURICIO *hará de Don Luis,* ROBERTO *de Don Juan.* ROBERTO *se sienta en una banqueta.* ELENA *le sirve un trago. Entra Don Luis.*

MAURICIO: Vive Dios ...

ROBERTO: (*Saliendo de situación.*) Ya empezaste mal.

MAURICIO: ¿Por qué?

ROBERTO: Hoy en día nadie dice »vive Dios».

MAURICIO: Tienes razón. Vamos a hacerlo otra vez.

Comienzan la escena de nuevo.

MAURICIO: ¡Vaya, mi pana, El Juanito!

ROBERTO: (*Interrumpiendo, saliéndose de situación de nuevo.*) Perdona Mauricio, pero eso de "pana" ... Aquí no se ha discutido si esta adaptación va a ser puertorriqueña o qué. A mí me parece que eso de "pana" nada más que lo entienden los puertorriqueños, y yo creo que la adaptación debe ser más universal. No podemos reducir el mercado.

MAURICIO: ¿A tí quién te entiende? ¿Quieres que lo hagamos en castellano, con las zetas ... ?

ROBERTO: No digo eso. Estoy diciendo que ...

ELENA: (*Interrumpiendo, exasperada.*) ¡Ay, caballeros, no jodan más con la lengua! ¡Que hable como sea, esto na' más que es una prueba, coño! (*Se persigna al darse cuenta que está haciendo de monja.*)

MAURICIO: Doña Inés tiene razón.

ROBERTO: Bueno, pues sigue.

Comienza la escena de nuevo.

MAURICIO: ¡Ah, aquí estás, Juan Tenorio! Veo que no has faltado a la cita.

ROBERTO: Soy hombre de palabra. Hace un año acordamos encontrarnos en este bar para cerrar nuestra apuesta, y aquí estoy. ¿Qué quieres tomar?

MAURICIO: Una Heineken.

ROBERTO: (*Saliéndose de situación.*) ¡Una Heineken! ¿Una Heineken? ¡Don Luis no tomaría una Heineken!

ELENA: (*Interrumpiendo, impaciente por continuar.*) Claro que sí. He aquí la Heineken. (*Pone la botella en el bar de un tirón.*) Sigan, por favor.

MAURICIO: (*Guiñándole un ojo a* ELENA.) Gracias, Doña.

ROBERTO: (ROBERTO *se pone de pie, súbitamente furioso.*) ¡Gracias, Doña! ¡Gracias, Doña! ¡Pero qué ridiculez, señores! ¡Si alguien nos viera por un agujero pensaría que estábamos locos! ¡Tal vez estamos locos! ¡Los efectos de la radiación en el cerebro! (ROBERTO *va hacia el televisor y lo enciende de un manotazo. Sólo se ve estática.*)

ELENA: Deja eso. Sabes muy bien que ningún canal está transmitiendo por el momento.

ROBERTO: ¿Por el momento? ¡Más nunca van a transmitir! ¿No lo entienden? ¡Más nunca habrá telenovelas! Estamos perdiendo el tiempo. ¡Es más, ya lo hemos perdido del todo!

MAURICIO: Quedamos en que no íbamos a hablar más de eso. Le das demasiada importancia al asunto. Las emisoras volverán a transmitir. Habrá cientos de nuevas telenovelas y nosotros seremos las estrellas. Cuando todo esto se resuelva los productores van a necesitar muchos guiones nuevos, y allí estaremos nosotros, ¡preparados!

ELENA: (*Quitándose el paño blanco de la cabeza va y apaga el televisor.*) Vamos a descansar un rato. Llevamos demasiadas horas en esto. No hay por qué apresurarse tanto.

ROBERTO *va hacia la ventana y entreabre las cortinas, mira hacia afuera.* MAURICIO *se sienta en el sofá con la cabeza entre las manos.* ELENA *busca en su cartera.*

ELENA: ¡Coño, se me acabaron los cigarrillos!

ROBERTO: (ROBERTO *se vuelve desde la ventana. La mira con incredulidad meneando la cabeza.*) Imagínense, el fin del mundo y nada que fumar.

MAURICIO: (*Levantando la cabeza sin moverse.*) Hay una onza de marihuana en la nevera. En el pomo de la mostaza.

ELENA: No, lo que quiero es un cigarrillo común y corriente.

ROBERTO: Ya no existe nada común y corriente. Ahora todo es extraordinario.

ELENA: No empieces con tus filosofías de baratillo. Voy a darme un baño y después continuamos con el guión. (ELENA *sale.*)

ROBERTO: (ROBERTO *coge un tocacintas portátil que hay sobre la mesa, se pone los audífonos y escucha por un rato.*) ¡Esto si que es una crisis! ¡El único cassette que tenemos y es de Julio Iglesias!

MAURICIO: A Elena se le olvidó traer la caja con los cassettes.

ROBERTO: No se por qué la invitaste. La casa de playa me la prestaron a MÍ y yo te invité a TI. Mi idea era pasar unos días tranquilos ... y mira en lo que ha parado todo esto.

MAURICIO: Ella no tiene la culpa de ... de lo que pasa allá afuera.

ROBERTO: TODOS tenemos la culpa de lo que pasa allá afuera ... pero, bueno, eso ya no tiene remedio. De todos modos, hubiera preferido que ella no viniera ...

MAURICIO: Tu invitación fue un poco vaga, Roberto. Me debías haber advertido que la invitación era para mí. Tu sabes que he estado saliendo con Elena desde que hicimos "Sin sombra". No sabía que su presencia te molestaba tanto.

ROBERTO: No es eso ... Elena y yo nos conocemos desde hace mucho tiempo. Han pasado cosas entre nosotros que prefiero olvidar ...

ELENA: (ELENA *entra, pálida de susto.*) No hay agua.

MAURICIO: ¿Cómo que no hay agua?

ELENA: No hay. Ni una gota.

MAURICIO: ¡No puede ser! (MAURICIO *sale corriendo hacia el interior.* ROBERTO *va hacia el bar y se sirve un trago con mucha tranquilidad.*)

ROBERTO: (*Tranquilo.*) No sé qué esperan ustedes.

MAURICIO: (MAURICIO *entra, pálido de terror.*) No hay agua. ¡Ni una gota! ¡Nos moriremos de sed!

ELENA: ¡Y oliendo mal!

ROBERTO: (*Tomando un sorbo de su trago.*) Pero hay tres botellas de ron, una de whisky, media de tequila, un chin chin de vodka y una de ginebra sin abrir.

ELENA: (ELENA *le arrebata el vaso de las manos a* ROBERTO. Lo tira contra la pared, semi histérica.) ¡Estoy harta de tu sorna! ¡De tu actitud de superioridad, de inteligencia, de raciocinio! ¡Este no es el momento para esas cosas! (ELENA *sale furiosamente.*)

MAURICIO: (MAURICIO *se arrastra hacia el sofá, como un sediento perdido en el desierto.*) Agua ... agua ... no hay agua. No hay ni una gota de agua. Me muero de sed. Tengo la garganta seca. Daría cualquier cosa ... cualquier cosa por un vaso de agua. Bien fría. Que entumezca los dientes. Un vaso de agua fría ... Ya lo veo ... debe ser un espejismo ... Un vaso sudado, con cubitos de hielo flotando en el líquido cristalino, cubitos de hielo haciendo clink, clink en el costado del vaso. (*Traga en seco.*) ... Agua, que cosa tan maravillosa, tan simple, tan humilde, tan refrescante ... un vaso de agua ... me muero por un vaso de agua ... (*Saca la lengua, llevándose las manos a la garganta.*)

ROBERTO: Antes tú nunca tomabas agua. Eras de la "Generación Pepsi", ¿te acuerdas? Hasta te desayunabas con la basofia esa.

MAURICIO: (*Saliéndose de situación.*) ¡No tienes por qué faltarme al respeto! Las cosas cambian, uno cambia. ¡Ahora me muero por un vaso de agua!

ELENA: (ELENA *entra en una silla de ruedas. Lleva el pelo envuelto en una toalla, como un turbante. Viste bata de casa. Coloca la silla de ruedas en el centro de la habitación. Habla con voz hipnotizante.*) Mauricio.

MAURICIO: (*Volviéndose hacia ella, como hipnotizado.*) Mande, señora.

ELENA: Ven, acércate. (MAURICIO *se acerca.*) Arrodíllate. (MAURICIO *se arrodilla. Ella le da un frasco de crema.*) Ponme crema en los pies .... (*Suspirando de placer.*) ... María me acaba de dar un baño que me ha hecho renacer.

MAURICIO: (MAURICIO *le pone crema. Se queda embelesado admirándole el pie.*) Señora ... ¿me permite besarlo?

ELENA: Bésalo, hijo, bésalo. ¡Cuántos labios famosos no han besado ese pie! Antes de mi accidente ... claro ... cuando yo era la prima ballerina más cotizada del mundo, príncipes sauditas, primeros ministros, banqueros, magnates navieros, violinistas ...

MAURICIO: Y ahora mis labios, los labios de un simple sirviente analfabeto ... (*Le besa el pie.*).

ROBERTO: (*Desde el bar, sirviéndose otro trago.*) Me acuerdo de esa. "El vals de la inválida". Ciento sesenta y seis capítulos. Primera en los "ratings" durante tres años. Yo hacía el papel de Renato. Como no me voy a acordar? Fue nuestra primera telenovela juntos.

MAURICIO: (MAURICIO *se pone de pie y va hacia el bar. Se sienta y se sirve un trago.*) No me perdí ni un solo capítulo. Yo era todavía un niño, pero mi mamá la veía todos los días. (MAURICIO *se estremece ligeramente. Se pasa las manos por los brazos descubiertos.*) ¿No sienten frío?

ELENA: Estamos en agosto.

ROBERTO: Eso era antes ... agosto, septiembre, octubre.

MAURICIO: Voy a buscar un suéter. (MAURICIO *sale al cuarto.*)

ROBERTO: (*Contemplando a* ELENA, *quien todavía está en la silla de ruedas. Se acerca, se le para detrás, se dirige a ella con gran sinceridad.*) Yo me enamoré de ti en esa silla de ruedas ... Por primera vez te vi diferente. Vulnerable. Sentí que, quizás, podrías necesitarme ... que quizás había algo que yo podía darte. Tú tan altiva, tan suficiente ... la inalcanzable estrella al alcance de mi mano ... Casi me lo creo. A veces eras tan sincera, tan real. Recuerdo la noche que te invité a escuchar mi colección de discos viejos. Puse uno de boleros, de esos "cortavenas" de victrolas de bares. Te dije: "no se si te gustarán estos vejestorios" ... y tú me contestaste: "vejestorios no ... ¡esos son himnos!" ... Ahí, me enamoré más todavía.

ELENA: (*Moviendo la silla de ruedas hacia el frente, alejándose un tanto de* ROBERTO. *Habla sin mirarlo.*) Tal vez fue por lástima. Una mujer bella y famosa, condenada a una silla de ruedas, ejerce un atractivo sobrenatural. Pero yo no quiero tu amor así, Renato. Prefiero la soledad. Prefiero vivir de mis recuerdos, de mi gloria pasada. Yo me siento aquí y revivo en mi mente los más gloriosos momentos ... aquella función de "El lago de los cisnes" en París ... "Las Sílfides" en Milán ... (*Rueda la silla hacia la ventana.*) Lo siento, Renato, pero comprenderás que el simple amor de un hombre como tú no puede competir con mi pasado legendario. Es mejor que me olvides. (*Se miran por un segundo.*)

MAURICIO *entra y mira primero a* ELENA, *después a* ROBERTO. ELENA *sale en la silla de ruedas.* MAURICIO *lleva un suéter y una toalla de bufanda.*

ROBERTO: (ROBERTO *se sirve otro trago y le sirve uno a Mauricio.*) Tómate uno conmigo. Vamos a ver si es verdad que la bebida ahoga las penas. A decir verdad, yo nunca lo he logrado. Mis penas parecen ser nadadoras olímpicas.

MAURICIO: Yo no se si ahoga las penas, pero si sé que la bebida hace entrar en calor. ¡Y yo tengo un frío! ... ¿Por qué hace tanto frío? ¿Qué pasó con el verano tropical?

ROBERTO: Olvida eso, nada de eso importa, nada, nada. El frío que llevo en el alma es mucho más grande. (*Medio borracho.*) Mauri ... las mujeres son unas castradoras. ¿Te das cuenta del problema de los hombres? La única mujer en la vida que vale la pena es nuestra madre. La única. Todas las demás son unas harpías. Nos hacen sufrir. Nos trituran las bolas.

MAURICIO: Nos joden la vida. Nos llevan al abismo. ¿Qué nos queda?

ROBERTO: Quedan los amigos .... Escúchame, Mauri ... Yo ... yo abandoné la farra y los amigos, porque ella me lo pidió. Me convertí en hombre de bien. Trabajador, responsable ... ¿Y para qué? ¿Para qué? Para que ella luego me abandonara por un hombre rico, un viejo millonario ... ¿Tú puedes creer eso?

MAURICIO: De las mujeres lo creo todo. Brindemos por las traidoras. (*Cantan canción de Felipe Rodríguez.*)

Y pasaron muchos años de ilusión
entregado a las delicias de mi amor
pero al fin he comprendido
vale más cualquier amigo
sea un borracho, sea un perdido
que la mas linda mujer

Durante la canción, ROBERTO *le ha echado el brazo por encima a* MAURICIO, *y le canta —sugestivamente— muy cerca del oído.* ELENA *entra y los sorprende.* ROBERTO *se retira rápidamente.* ELENA *va hacia la ventana y mira por entre las persianas.*

ELENA: Hay un viento tremendo en la playa. Las olas están que dan miedo. (ELENA *se retira de la ventana y se sienta en el sofá.*)

ROBERTO: No sé cómo puedes ver en la oscuridad ... Hace tres días que estamos en la oscuridad total. Tres días en que no vemos el sol .... ¿No les hace falta?

ELENA: (*Revisando unos libros y revistas que hay sobre la mesa.*) A mí nunca me ha gustado el sol. No es bueno para la piel. Da pecas. Envejece. Da cáncer. (*Tirando un libro con desprecio.*) ¡En esta casa no hay nada que leer!

ROBERTO: ¿Y esos libros para qué son? ¿Para comer?

MAURICIO: Pues, mira, pudiera ser, porque ya casi no queda comida . . .

ELENA: Quiero decir revistas de moda . . . de la farándula, un TeVe Guía . . . una Radiolandia . . .

ROBERTO: El dueño de esta casa no leía esas cosas. Era un hombre muy bien informado. Por eso cuando empezó la crisis, cogió un avión y se largó a Nueva Zelandia. Pensó que allí tendría un chance de salvarse.

MAURICIO: (*Nervioso.*) ¡Ya están con eso otra vez!

ROBERTO: (*Sarcástico.*) Si no quieres oírlo, ¿por qué no te vas a dar una vuelta? ¿O a la playa, a echar una nadadita? ¿O a dormir la siesta bajo el cocotero? Anda, ve.

ELENA: Y tú, ¿por qué no haces una cita con tu exorcista?

ROBERTO: (ROBERTO *va hacia el teléfono, lo levanta, marca un número.*) ¡Hola! ¡Hola! . . . Con el Padre Antonio, por favor. ¿Oigo? ¿Oigo? . . . . (*Irónico.*) ¡Qué raro, el teléfono no funciona! ¡Qué raro, no hay agua! ¡Qué raro! . . .

ELENA: (*Le arrebata el teléfono de la mano.*) ¿Cómo que no funciona? ¡Claro que funciona! (*Aprieta el botón de enganchar y lo vuelve a soltar. Marca un número.*) Claro que funciona, ya verás . . . está dando timbre . . . ¿Hola? . . . ¿Es la Señora Roselló? ¿Sabe quién le habla? . . . ¿No? . . . Soy . . . soy "la otra", ja, ja, ja. La llamo para decirle que Mauricio se va conmigo, yo soy la que él ama. El me adora, ¿me entiende? ¡Me adora! . . . ¿Eso? . . . no tiene importancia. En el amor la edad no importa. El será más joven que yo, pero yo sé darle lo que una chiquilla inocente como tú no puede darle. (*Acaricia el cabello de* MAURICIO , *quien ha venido a sentarse cerca de ella.*) ¿Mala yo? . . . Sí, soy "mala", siempre me ha tocado ser la mala, la villana de la película. Querida mía, las mujeres "buenas" no llegan a nada . . . a nada más que a viejas gordas, solas y frustradas. No me asusta la posibilidad del infierno, porque los años que he vivido en la tierra han sido el paraíso . . . (*Escucha. Hace una mueca de asco.*) . . . Quitarse la vida es una cobardía, un acto de mal gusto, pero si insistes te recomiendo las pastillas . . . es un método menos dramático, pero más higiénico. (*Cuelga el teléfono con un gesto victorioso. Sonríe, satisfecha con su actuación.* ROBERTO *aplaude.* MAURICIO , *intrigado, le quita el auricular de las manos a* ELENA. *Se lo pone al oído. Se da cuenta que no hay tono de discar, lo cual lo desconcierta visiblemente.*)

ROBERTO: ¡Brava, bravísima! ¿"Amor de Otoño"?

ELENA: No, "Mujer sin Alma". Doscientos capítulos.

ROBERTO: ¡Ah, es verdad! No me acordaba. En esa fuiste mala de verdad.

ELENA: Sí, la dragona en celo echando fuego por todos los agujeros.

MAURICIO: (*Tratando de disimular su desconcierto.*) Elena, ¿recuerdas aquel productor amigo tuyo, el cubano de Miami? Ése es un buen contacto. Le enviaremos el guión a él, primero que a nadie.

ROBERTO: ¿Para qué? En los Estados Unidos no hacen telenovelas en español. Allá nada más que ven las porquerías que hacemos aquí.

ELENA: Roberto, no hables así. Aquí se han hecho telenovelas que no tienen nada que envidiarle a "Dynasty". Obras maestras del género.

ROBERTO: (*Despectivamente, sirviéndose otro trago.*) ¡Ja!

ELENA: ¿Tú me quieres decir a mí que "La bella malvada", mi papel cumbre, no fue una obra maestra? ¿Y qué me dices de "Mátame, pero no me abandones"? Con esa me gané la Palmera de Oro. Y eso que allí hacía de "buena", o sea, de víctima.

MAURICIO: Me acuerdo de esa. Viéndola es que decidí ser actor de televisión. Mi mamá tuvo mucha influencia en eso también. Yo era tan lindo desde que nací, que ella decía que esta cara debía de admirarla el mundo entero ... Me puso Mauricio, porque ése era el nombre de su personaje favorito en "La mujer sin pasado." Mi sueño siempre ha sido este ... ser actor de televisión ... Uno se siente admirado, querido, uno se convierte en parte de la vida diaria de tanta gente ... entra en sus hogares ... los ayuda a que no piensen en la realidad, a olvidarse de la miseria que les rodea ... Sí, uno existe mas allá de uno mismo ...

ELENA: Por supuesto que sí, es algo muy especial. Uno vive vidas diferentes. Muere muertes dramáticas, espectaculares.

ROBERTO: (*Con sorna.*) Muy distinto a la vida real, ¿no es verdad? En la vida real, la mayoría de las vidas y las muertes son aburridas, rutinarias, pasan por desapercibidas ...

ELENA: (*Intensa.*) Roberto, ¿tú crees que yo no me doy cuenta que la mayoría de las telenovelas son estúpidas, que entretienen a la gente con historias que no tienen nada que ver con la realidad? Claro que lo sé. Pero, ¿qué quieres que haga? Yo no tengo la energía necesaria para cambiar el mundo. Yo también tuve mis aspiraciones y mis sueños reales. ¿Tú no crees que como actriz no he querido hacer grandes papeles en el teatro, en películas? Papeles épicos, con mensajes que iluminen y hagan pensar a la humanidad. ¡Claro que he querido! Tú no eres el único que estudió "el método", querido. Yo estudié, me preparé, invertí mucho tiempo y dinero en talleres de actuación, de elocución, de expresión corporal. Pero la oportunidad nunca tocó a mi puerta. Esto es lo que me ha tocado hacer en la vida —telenovelas, melodramas para amas de casa— y lo hago lo mejor que puedo, con dignidad, con la barbilla en alto, dándole la espalda al pasado, a las ruinas de mis sueños ... a lo que pudo haber sido ... (*Pausa silenciosa. Todos se miran.*)

ROBERTO: No recuerdo de cuál telenovela es ese monólogo. (ROBERTO *sale.*)

ELENA: (*Con furia contenida.*) ¡Ayy! ¡Si tuviera los ovarios bien puestos, lo asesinaría un día de estos!

MAURICIO: (*A* ELENA.) No le hagas caso. Ha bebido mucho.

ELENA: No es sólo la bebida. Es un amargado, un frustrado. Siempre quiso ser lo que no es. Siempre se ha creído superior a los demás. Un actor serio venido a menos, un actor de gran escenario reducido a la pantalla pequeña.

MAURICIO: No seas tan dura con él. Voy a ver que le pasa. (MAURICIO *sale.*)

ELENA: (ELENA, *enfurecida, lo sigue unos pasos, grita trás él.*) ¡Sí, corre! ¡Corre a lamerle las heridas! ¿Ustedes se creen que yo no me doy cuenta de lo que está pasando? Llevo muchos años en la farándula para no darme cuenta. ¡No será la primera vez que un hombre me quita el marido! ¡Ni la última! ¡He pasado por todo en la vida, por todo! ¡Sé arreglármelas muy bien sola! (*Se calma. Camina por la habitación, examinando los muebles y las paredes con el tacto. Llega frente al espejo que está colgado en la pared, sobre el televisor.*) ... Sola ... toda una vida de aventuras pasajeras ... de romances con caras y cuerpos bellos ... con los galanes más cotizados ... noches de cabaret y de champán, de ilusiones pretendidas ... pero, en fin, sola ... sólo el espejo sabe la verdad ... (*Comienza a agacharse hasta que su cara queda reflejada en la pantalla apagada del televisor.*) ... Quién soy ... qué edad tengo, cómo me llamo ... adónde voy ... de qué color es mi pelo en realidad ... pero ya nada de eso importa ... ahora que ... ahora que estoy ... ¡ciega!

MAURICIO: (MAURICIO, *quien ha entrado unas líneas antes y la ha estado observando, decide entrar en el juego.*) ¿La señora ... Carnevale?

ELENA: (*Se vuelve hacia* MAURICIO , *con las manos extendidas frente a sí, como una ciega.*) ¿Quién es? ¿Qué hace aquí?

MAURICIO: Vengo a arreglar el televisor. Perdone la demora, pero es que tenemos mucho trabajo en el taller. Medio pueblo tiene los televisores rotos .... A ver, cuál es es el problema ... (*Va hacia el televisor y lo vira al revés, como para mirarlo por dentro.*)

ELENA: Su voz me es tan familiar. Déjeme tocarle la cara para ver ... sentir ... si lo conozco ... (*Le toca la cara con las dos manos, baja hacia el cuello, luego al pecho. Sus manos se detienen en una medalla que* MAURICIO *lleva colgada del cuello. La toca con mucho interés. Abre los ojos y la mira con curiosidad, saliéndose de situación.*) Mauricio ... ¿Y esa medalla? Nunca te la había visto.

MAURICIO: No sé de dónde salió. La llevo desde que tengo uso de razón. Las monjitas del orfelinato donde me crié me hicieron prometer que nunca me la quitaría.

ELENA: (*Visiblemente alterada y nerviosa.*) ¡No ... no lo puedo creer! Imposible ... Después de tantos años ...

MAURICIO: Elena, ¿qué te sucede? Estás pálida, te sudan las manos ... parece que has visto un fantasma.

ELENA: Un fantasma, sí. El fantasma de mi pasado. Mauricio ... tengo algo que confesarte. Esa ... esa medalla que llevas puesta al cuello ... es ... es mía.

MAURICIO: ¡No puede ser! La llevo desde pequeño. Ni siquiera te conocía.

ELENA: Sí, sí me conocías. Esa medalla es mía, yo te la colgué al cuello cuando te dejé, una mañana fría y lluviosa, en los escalones del hospicio. Aquella mañana casi muero de dolor y de frío ... frío en el alma por lo que acababa de hacer ... Mauricio, hijo, no sé si algún día podrás perdonarme.

MAURICIO: (*Confundido.*) ¿Hijo? ... ¿Perdonarte? ... No entiendo lo que quieres decir, Elena ...

ELENA: No vuelvas a llamarme Elena, te lo ruego. Llámame con el nombre que hace tantos años deseo escuchar de tus labios ... ¡madre!

MAURICIO: (*Con el rostro iluminado de alegría.*) ¡Madre! (*Se abrazan.*)

Entra ROBERTO *envuelto en una sábana a manera de toga romana. A mitad del discurso,* MAURICIO *se pondrá los audífonos para no escucharlo.*

ROBERTO: (*A la manera de un actor "shakesperiano."*) ¡Madre! ¡Padre! ¡Hermanos, prestadme atención! ¡Vengo a sepultar a César, no a ensalzarle! ¡El mal que hacen los hombres perdura sobre su memoria! ¡Frecuentemente el bien queda enterrado con sus huesos! El mundo es una pantalla, y sobre ella vemos proyectada la telenovela de nuestros tiempos, capítulo a capítulo. El tiempo apremia. Nos encontramos al borde del abismo, en el ojo mismo de la tormenta. Ya no queda la esperanza del mañana. Nos queda hoy la certeza de este único y fugaz momento. Es hora de cerrar nuestras casas de campaña, de empaquetar nuestras armas y decir adiós. Algunos de nosotros hicimos lo más que pudimos por ganar esta batalla, por alertar a la humanidad de los peligros que la acechaban. Pero sólo encontramos indiferencia, ignorancia, supersticiones, desconfianza .... Ya es muy tarde para recriminaciones. De nada valdrían. Marchemos hacia la extinción, como las grandes bestias de los tiempos primordiales, como erguidos dinosaurios, contentos en el saber que fuimos las más grandes, las más poderosas criaturas que pisaron la tierra. Marchemos, como hurones, hacia el exterminio una vez más, tranquilos en la certeza de que en un futuro muy lejano, nuestros huesos serán admirados en los museos, y de que nuestra desaparición será tema de disertaciones doctorales ... Arrastrémonos hacia la destrucción, convencidos de que no hemos existido en vano, seguros de que nuestra fugaz presencia sobre el planeta ha tenido un propósito, a pesar de que en la historia del universo éste ha sido, simplemente, un momento más ...

ELENA: (ELENA *da un grito de loca.*) ¡No! ¡No puedo más! ¡Esto es un manicomio! ¡No resisto oír una palabra más. ¡Basta, basta! ¡Prefiero morir ahora mismo que vivir en este mundo alucinante con dos locos peligrosos! ¡Voy a cortarme las venas! ¡Quiero cortarme las venas! ¡Denme algo con qué cortarme las venas! ¡Un cuchillo, una navaja, una gem, un machete ... ! (*Busca como una loca por todos los rincones de la casa. Encuentra unas tijeras enormes.*

Trata de cortarse las muñecas de un tijeretazo.)

ROBERTO: Elena, ¿qué haces? ¡Dame acá esas tijeras!

MAURICIO *y* ROBERTO, *asustados, tratan de arrebatarle las tijeras de la mano.* ELENA *se enfurece más aún y comienza a apuñalearlos con las tijeras.* ROBERTO *cae en el sofá, se tapa la cabeza con la sábana tratando de protegerse. Ella lo apuñala despiadadamente, él da un grito de muerte.* ELENA *persigue a* MAURICIO *por toda la habitación.*

ELENA: ¡Tú también, tú también, Príncipe de la Noche! ¡Tú también, Cara Linda!

MAURICIO: ¡Elena, te has vuelto loca, deja esas tijeras! ¡Es sólo un juego!

ELENA: ¡No, no es un juego, ya nada es un juego! Ya todo es un juego. ¡Lo único que queda es el juego! (ELENA *alcanza a* MAURICIO *y le entierra las tijeras por la espalda.* MAURICIO *cae lentamente en una muerte de película.* ELENA *se arrodilla junto a él y lo acuna en sus brazos. Suave.*) ¿Hijo . . . ? ¿Hijito, me escuchas? Te dejé en el hospicio porque no podía tenerte. Una actriz como yo, siempre viajando, viviendo y muriendo en los escenarios más pobres y polvorientos de las provincias. ¿Qué vida era esa para un niño tan lindo como tú? Perdóname . . . perdóname . . . (*Llora bajito.*)

MAURICIO: (MAURICIO *abre los ojos, con gran esfuerzo abre la boca para hablar.*) Elena . . .

ELENA: Dime, hijo de mi alma. Quiero escuchar tus últimas palabras.

MAURICIO: Sancocho.

ELENA: ¿Sancocho?

MAURICIO: (*Poniéndose de pie.*) Sí, chica, muchas cosas diferentes revueltas en la misma olla. Además, demasiado melodramático. ¿Tú no crees, Roberto?

ROBERTO: (*Sin salir de debajo de la sábana.*) Yo no sé por qué siempre caemos en la misma mierda.

ELENA: Ustedes me van a perdonar, pero estoy totalmente en desacuerdo con ustedes. No me pueden negar que la escena de las tijeras es *bastante* original.

MAURICIO: Sí . . . creo que solo la he visto una decena de veces. Pero tengo que confesarte que por un momento me asustaste de verdad. Pensé que habías perdido la cabeza.

ELENA: (*Con satisfacción.*) Sí, la verdad es que me quedó muy bien, ¿no? (*Pausa.*) Bueno . . . ¿y ahora qué hacemos?

ROBERTO: (*Debajo de la sábana.*) Ya estoy cansado de este jueguito. Quiero descansar en paz ... y resucitar a los siete días cuando ya el mundo esté hecho de nuevo.

ELENA: (MAURICIO *se pone los audífonos del casette otra vez.*) Ya se está poniendo morboso otra vez.

MAURICIO: Olvida eso. Ven, vamos a bailar.

Cada uno se pone uno de los audífonos y comienza a bailar. Bailan un rato con las cabezas muy juntas, pensativamente. De repente ELENA *se quita su audífono.*

ELENA: Mauricio, ¿sabes qué ... ?

MAURICIO: (*Quitándose su audífono.*) ¿Qué?

ELENA: Fíjate, estoy un poco cansada de la seriedad de las telenovelas ... tanto lloriqueo, tanto sufrimiento, tanta intriga. ¿Por qué no puede haber telenovelas cómicas ... o con música?

MAURICIO: Pues ... a nadie se le habrá ocurrido ...

ELENA: A ver que te parece esta idea: A mí se me ocurre una telenovela-opereta, pero con música popular. Todo cantado, con boleros que se ajusten a la ocasión.

MAURICIO: ¿Por ejemplo?

ELENA: Por ejemplo ... (*Piensa un poco. Se le ocurre una idea. Canta.*) "Y tú, ¿cómo estás?"

MAURICIO: (*Cantando.*) "¿Yo? ... Encantado de la vida. Y tú, ¿cómo estás?"

ELENA: (*Cantando.*) "Yo, encantada del amor".

MAURICIO: (*Cantando.*) "¿Cómo fue? ... "

ELENA: (*Cantando.*) "No sé explicarme como fue. Fueron sus ojos o su boca. Fueron sus manos o su piel. Fue a lo mejor la impaciencia de tanto esperar ... "

MAURICIO: (MAURICIO *se ríe y aplaude.*) ¡Qué lindo! ¡Me gusta la idea! Roberto, Roberto, ¿estás escuchando?

ROBERTO: (*Cantando, debajo de la sábana.*) "Adiós muchachos, compañeros de mi vida, farras queridas de aquellos tiempos. Me toca a mi hoy emprender la retirada ... "

ELENA: (*Cantando, metiéndose debajo de la sábana con* ROBERTO.) "Este amor apasionado, anda todo alborotado, por volver ... "

ROBERTO: "Déjame, no quiero que me toques. Por tu culpa estoy sufriendo, la tortura del recuerdo."

MAURICIO: (MAURICIO *se quita la camisa y se mete debajo de la sábana. Canta.*) "Dame un beso y olvida que me has besado. Yo te ofrezco la vida si me la pides ... "

Los tres siguen cantando debajo de la sábana. Uno a uno dejan de cantar y se oyen sonidos sugerentes y sensuales. Las luces bajan paulatinamente hasta llegar a un apagón total. En la oscuridad se escucha el rugir del viento en la playa. Al subir las luces de nuevo los tres están en el sofá. Sus hombros desnudos se ven sobre el borde de la sábana. Comparten un cigarrillo de marihuana.

MAURICIO: Me comería una pizza con peperoni.
ELENA: Y yo un un bistec encebollado con papas fritas.
MAURICIO: No, mejor una carne guisada con arroz blanco y tostones.
ELENA: Y de postre, fresas con crema.
MAURICIO: Melocotones en almíbar.
ELENA: Café vienés.
ROBERTO: Yo me comería ... dos chuletas de cerdo ...
ELENA: Pero, ¿y tú no eras vegetariano?
ROBERTO: Sí, pero ahora que sé que más nunca podré comer chuletas, daría un brazo por una.
ELENA: Mejor sería algo que nunca se ha probado. A ver ...
MAURICIO: ... Caviar ... yo nunca he comido caviar.
ELENA: No te has perdido nada del otro mundo. Es muy salado.
ROBERTO: Fíjate, no había pensado en eso ...
MAURICIO: ¿En qué?
ROBERTO: En todas las cosas que nunca he hecho. Por ejemplo ... yo nunca he jugado al golf.
ELENA: Es un juego de viejos.
ROBERTO: Nunca he estado en París.
ELENA: Yo nunca he estado en Japón.
ROBERTO: Nunca subí a los Andes.
ELENA: Nunca sembré un árbol.
ROBERTO: Nunca me bañe en un río.
ELENA: Nunca caminé descalza en la nieve.
ROBERTO: Nunca le cambié los pañales a un bebé.
ELENA: Nunca di a luz a un bebé.
ROBERTO: Nunca ...
MAURICIO: (MAURICIO *se levanta muy alterado.*) ¡Nunca he pescado un marlín! ¡Nunca he cazado mariposas! ¡Nunca he levantado una pared con mis propias manos! Ustedes no habrán hecho muchas cosas, pero han hecho más que yo. ¡Yo sólo tengo 22 años! ¡Me falta mucho por vivir! ¡Me falta enamorarme de verdad! ¡Me falta subir montañas! ¡Me falta que me salgan canas! ¡Todavía ni siquiera he leído *Cién años de soledad*! ... ¡Nunca!

¡Nunca! ¡Nunca! ¡No lo acepto! ¡No lo puedo aceptar! ¡No es justo que algún viejo haya apretado un botón y haya mandado todo al carajo! ¡Nunca! ¿Saben lo que nunca podré aceptar? ¡Que el mundo esté dominado por viejos decrépitos, llenos de ideas decrépitas!

ELENA *se levanta y va hacia el televisor. Lo enciende, el volumen de la estática ahoga las últimas palabras de* MAURICIO . *Hay un frío intenso. El aire se ha enrarecido.* ROBERTO *apaga el televisor.*

ROBERTO: Demasiado fuerte. Demasiado realista, Mauricio. No puede haber tanto desborde de pasión frente a las cámaras. Ademas, es un monólogo muy vago. ¿De qué hablas? ¿Cuál es el motivo de tu explosión emocional? No, no creo que lo podemos usar.

MAURICIO: (*Lo ignora. Se pone los audífonos. Le da vuelta a los botones. Tose.*) Parece que se gastaron las baterías.

ELENA: ¿Cuánto tiempo nos quedará?

ROBERTO: Toda una vida. (*Se pasa las manos por el pelo y nota que se le está cayendo.*) Ya se me está cayendo el pelo. (*Subrepticiamente,* MAURICIO *también se pasa la mano por el pelo y se la mira. Larga pausa silenciosa.*)

ELENA: (*Pensativa.*) Yo no fuí una buena hija, ¿saben? Ignoraba a mis padres. Pensaba que no eran sofisticados, que nada de lo que decían tenía importancia. Mi mamá sólo hablaba de sus enfermedades. Mi papá siempre hacía los mismos chistes. Y se emborrachaba.

ROBERTO: Mis padres no querían que yo fuera actor. No lo tomaban en serio como profesión. "Eso es cosa de maricones", me decía el viejo. Se murió de una hernia por levantar cajas demasiado pesadas para él.

MAURICIO: Mi mamá se creía todo lo que veía en la televisión . . .

ELENA: (*Las luces comienzan a parpadear, disminuyen en intensidad.*) En la cocina hay unas velas.

ROBERTO: Las voy a buscar.

ELENA: (MAURICIO *se sienta al lado de* ELENA. *Ella lo abraza como si fuera un niño pequeño.*) No hay que temerle a la oscuridad, mi amor. Si piensas que estás en el mismo sitio, rodeado de las mismas cosas que estaban allí cuando las podías ver, no te dará miedo.

MAURICIO: (*Como un niño.*) No le tengo miedo a la oscuridad, mami. Pero me aburro sin la televisión. No hay nada que hacer en la oscuridad.

ELENA: Puedes jugar a imaginarte cosas, gente, lugares. Es como si pasaras una cinta de video por la mente.

Las luces parpadean de nuevo, bajan más de intensidad. La habitación está ahora en penumbras. ROBERTO *entra con una vela encendida.*

MAURICIO: Me imagino que ... que mañana saldrá el sol igual que antes. Que podré salir a la playa ...

ROBERTO: Yo me imagino que estoy en el barco con Pepe, y salimos a pescar a las seis de la mañana ... el mar está como un plato, el sol todavía no calienta. Yo remo, él habla de béisbol ...

ELENA: Yo me imagino que tengo 13 años ... que estoy en mi casa, en mi cuarto, sentada en mi escritorio ... y escribo en mi diario ... Querido diario: Hoy, viernes 15 de marzo él me miró y me sonrió ... y por poco me revienta el corazón ...

MAURICIO: Imagino que ... no ha pasado nada ... que todo era como antes ...

ROBERTO: Me imagino que me siento con mi hijo y le explico los ríos y los desiertos, los lagos y las montañas, la redondez de la tierra, una a una le señalo las maravillas de la naturaleza ... (*Tose.*).

ELENA: Me imagino que toda la casa huele a ajo fresco machacado ... que la abuela prepara mi sopa favorita ... . Me imagino que todavía puedo recordar como huele el ajo fresco machacado ... (*Tose.*)

MAURICIO: Imagino que soy un actor de televisión, que llego al estudio y me están esperando los compañeros, el director, los camarógrafos, la maquillista. Me imagino que vamos a comenzar a filmar el último capítulo de "Pasión Invernal" ... (*Le da un ataque de tos.*)

Las luces se apagan por completo. ELENA *enciende varias velas. Lleva una hacia la mesa que está frente al sofá. Al quedar iluminada la sala de nuevo vemos que* ELENA *está sola en escena y lleva una máscara de gas, la cual le da un aspecto de insecto.*

ELENA: (*Contempla la vela encendida. Suspira.*) Las velas son tan románticas.

ROBERTO: (*También lleva máscara.*) Excepto cuando hay que usarlas por necesidad.

ELENA: Hola, querido. Llegas temprano hoy.

ROBERTO: Y el niño, ¿dónde está?

MAURICIO: (*Entrando, también con una máscara.*) Aquí estoy, papá. Me siento más mal ...

ROBERTO: Será el catarro que anda por ahí. Abrígate bien ... Querida, te tengo una sorpresa. Cierra los ojos.

ELENA: (*Se cubre los ojos por encima de la máscara.*) ¿Qué será?

ROBERTO: Ábrelos. ¡Feliz aniversario! (*Le entrega un plumero de desempolvar como si fuera un ramo de flores.*)

ELENA: ¡Qué rosas tan bellas! ¡Mis favoritas! Pensé que se te había olvidado.

ROBERTO: Nunca olvido nuestros aniversarios. (*Se besan con las máscaras puestas. El rugido del viento aumenta.*)

ELENA: (*Tosiendo.*) He preparado una cena exquisita con tus platos favoritos.

ROBERTO: (*Tosiendo.*) ¡Qué maravilla! Vamos a abrir esa botella de vino francés que tenemos guardada para una ocasión especial. (*Saca una botella de vino, sirve dos copas. Hacen un brindis.*)

ELENA: Sabes, querido ... soy tan feliz.

ROBERTO: Yo también, mi amor.

Ambos se quedan inmóviles en el gesto del brindis. MAURICIO *, quien está sentado en el suelo mirando una vela fijamente, se vuelve a mirarlos, luego mira hacia el público. Se quita la máscara. Medio saliéndose de la situación, tosiendo, confundido, pero al mismo tiempo, a sí mismo.*

MAURICIO: Pero ... y esto ... ¿quién lo va a entender?

ELENA: (*Saliendo del "freeze", se quita la máscara. Habla faltándole el aliento.*) Nadie lo va a entender. No me gusta nada.

ROBERTO: (*Se quita la máscara. Tose.*) A mí tampoco.

MAURICIO: ¿Y qué hacemos?

ELENA: Lo que necesitamos son ideas frescas, nuevas ...

ROBERTO: Sí, eso, ideas nuevas ...

ELENA: Se está haciendo tarde ... A ver, ¿quién tiene una nueva idea?

Los tres se vuelven a poner las máscaras. Se sientan muy juntos en el piso de cara al público. Iluminados por las velas, sólo queda la imagen fosforecente de las tres máscaras en la oscuridad y el sonido amplificado de la respiración entrecortada de los tres. Las velas se apagan.

Fin

BOTÁNICA

Una comedia de milagros
1990

Botánica

PERSONAJES

DOÑA GENO. Genoveva Domínguez. Sesenta y tantos años. Nació en Guayama, Puerto Rico. Vive en Nueva York hace más de 40 años. Viuda. Es la dueña y señora de la Botánica La Ceiba, localizada en el área de Manhattan (Nueva York) conocida como El Barrio.

ANAMÚ. Cuarentona. Hija de Doña Geno. Divorciada. Es la madre de Milagros (Millie). Mujer indecisa, algo hastiada de la vida. Nació en Puerto Rico, pero llegó a Nueva York de niña.

MILLIE. Milagros Castillo. 22 años. Nacida en Nueva York. Se acaba de graduar de la universidad en Administración de Negocios.

RUBÉN. Veintiseis años. Amigo de Millie desde que eran niños. Nacido en Nueva York. Trabaja en una organización de desarrollo de la comunidad en El Barrio.

PEPE EL INDIO. De edad y nacionalidad incierta. Es un "homeless" borracho y filósofo que deambula por el vecindario.

LUISA y CARMEN. Clientas de la botánica.

SANTA BÁRBARA Y SAN LÁZARO. Dos santos.

ESCENOGRAFÍA

Toda la acción ocurre dentro de la Botánica La Ceiba. Aunque la escenografía no tiene que ser realista, sí es necesario que aparezca una cierta cantidad de parafernalia que se vende en las botánicas: velas, yerbas, incienso, frascos de esencia y despojos, aerosoles e imágenes de santos. Un enorme grabado o dibujo de una ceiba domina la escena. Debajo de ésta se encuentra la silla-trono de Doña Geno. A un lado hay un pequeño mostrador. Una puerta comunica con la calle, otra con el interior de la casa.

Botánica was commissioned and first produced by Teatro Repertorio Español. The first performance took place in New York City, on January 15, 1991 with the following cast:

DOÑA GENO .... Ofelia González
ANAMÚ .... Ana Margarita Martínez-Casado
MILLIE .... Ileana Guibert
RUBÉN .... Rolando Gómez
PEPE EL INDIO .... Juan Villarreal
CARMEN .... Marielva Sieg
LUISA .... Irma Bello

It was directed by Manuel Martín, Jr. Sets and costumes by Randy Barceló. Producers: René Buch, Roberto Federico and Gilberto Zaldívar for Repertorio Español.

PRIMER ACTO

Al subir las luces, DOÑA GENOVEVA *está atendiendo a una clienta en la botánica.*

LUISA: No creo que sea otra mujer, Doña Geno. ¿Con qué tiempo? El pobre tiene dos trabajos. Primero pensé que era por el pelo, usted sabe...

GENO: ¿Qué pelo?

LUISA: Mi pelo. Hace unos meses se me empezó a caer, perdió el brillo, se me puso como muerto – yo que tenía una maranta de pelo preciosa. Pero yo ví en la televisión, en los "Cinco Minutos con Mirta de Perales", que una señora le escribió contándole que su marido ya ni la miraba porque tenía el pelo feo. Mirta le recomendó su Loción Mirta, y zás, el pelo se le puso bello y el marido se volvió a enamorar de ella. Yo me compré la misma loción, pero nada. Arturo ni me mira. ¿Qué me recomienda usted, Doña Geno?

GENO: Sábila. Los americanos la llaman Aloe Vera. La tengo en líquido, en gelatina y en cápsulas.

LUISA: ¿Para el pelo?

GENO: (*Sacando botellas, cajas y sobres de sábila y poniéndolos sobre el mostrador.*) Hija, está comprobado que la sábila contiene propiedades medicinales para el tratamiento de artritis, presión alta, asma, vaginitis, disentería, erisipela, hemorroides, pie de atleta, salpullido, colitis, diarrea, estreñimiento, gripe, apoplejía, caspa, dolor de muelas, y ... (*Triunfante.*) ¡caída del cabello! ... Pero eso no es todo, la sábila es además un limpiador, refrescante, humectante y nutriente de la piel; estimula el páncreas, repele los insectos y elimina el mal olor de los pies, ayuda a bajar de peso, acondiciona el cabello ... y es un poderoso estimulante del poder sexual.

LUISA: ¡Ay Virgen! ¡Déme seis de líquido, seis de gelatina y cuatro de cápsulas!

GENO: (*Saca un sobre de manila.*) Por si las moscas, te recomiendo que quemes este incienso del "Perpetuo Socorro" varias veces al día, y cuando te bañes echa unas gotitas de este "Vente Conmigo Despojo Bath" en la bañera. Este lo preparo yo misma. Además te voy a dar una receta espiritual para traer buena suerte a la casa. Escucha bien: Coges un huevo, lo cruzas con una cinta blanca y una azul, le pones unas gotas del perfume que usas . . .

LUISA: Mirta.

GENO: . . . pones el huevo en un plato y le enciendes una vela roja, rezas tres Padres Nuestros y apagas la vela. Pon el huevo durante toda la noche a los pies de la cama. Al otro día lo levantas y lo tiras al río.

LUISA: ¿Cuál río?

GENO: Cualquiera.

LUISA: Creo que lo voy a tirar al Hudson. Es más grande.

GENO: El Hudson está bien, pero tíralo hacia downtown. Por allá arriba los dominicanos lo tienen un poco recargado.

LUISA: Ay, no sabe cuanto se lo agradezco, Doña Geno. ¿Cuánto le debo?

GENO: (GENO *arranca un pedazo de una bolsa de papel, escribe con un lápiz casi sin punta. Saca cuenta moviendo los labios.*) Son $45.50.

LUISA: Ay, fíjese, no pensé que sería tanto. No traigo tanto dinero conmigo.

GENO: No te preocupes, m'ijita. Dame lo que puedas. Lo otro te lo apunto y luego me lo traes.

LUISA: (LUISA *le da cinco dólares.* GENO *hace anotación en el pedazo de cartucho y lo echa en un shopping bag de papel que tiene sobre el mostrador.*) Sin falta se lo traigo en cuanto me pegue en la bolita esta semana. Otra consultita, Doña Geno: anoche soñé con Elsie. ¿Qué número cree que debo jugar?

GENO: ¿Quién es Elsie?

LUISA: La vaca de la televisión. ¿No se acuerda?

GENO: Ah, sí. Bueno, si soñaste que *viste* una vaca, eso significa que te van a visitar parientes. Si soñaste que estabas *ordeñando* una vaca, eso quiere decir que vas a ganar dinero

LUISA: No me acuerdo si la ordeñé o no.

GENO: De todos modos, juega el 744.

LUISA: El 744 . . . jmmm, suena lindo . . . Oiga, Doña Geno, ¿en cuánto tiempo usted cree que esto otro surta efecto?

GENO: Dale como dos semanas al asunto. Y déjame saber en cuanto notes algún cambio.

LUISA: Gracias, Doña Geno. Que Dios se lo pague. Adiós.

GENO: Hasta luego, m'ija, que Dios te bendiga. (*Se sienta en su silla debajo de la ceiba. Se echa fresco con un abanico de paja.*)

ANAMÚ: Mamá, por favor, vé y échale un ojo a la masa. Creo que me quedó demasiado monga. Y fíjate en la cantidad. Me parece poca. No sé si dará para cincuenta. De una vez pruébala de sal, quizás esté algo sosa.

GENO: Ay, m'ija, me acabo de sentar ...

ANAMÚ: Bueno ... cuando puedas ...

GENO: Cualquiera diría que es la primera vez que haces pasteles.

ANAMÚ: Es que estos pasteles me dan mala espina. No sé si es buena idea aparecernos allá cargadas de pasteles congelados.

GENO: ¿Tú crees que a esos gringos de Nu Jamprish no le van a gustar los pasteles? Ahí na' más que comen mitlof y papas salcochadas ...

ANAMÚ: Mamá, no todos son de New Hampshire. Hay gente de todas partes.

GENO: Bueno, si los gringos no los quieren, Milagritos se los come sola. Siempre le gustaron mucho los pasteles. Aunque últimamente le ha cogido un no sé qué a los tostones. La última vez que estuvo aquí estaba muy miquistiqui con la comida y no sé qué embelecos vegetarianos. ¡Como si los plátanos no fueran vegetales!

ANAMÚ: Mamá, es que a ella nunca le ha gustado el mofongo de desayuno.

GENO: Anamú, estás exagerando. ¿Cuándo he servido mofongo de desayuno?

ANAMÚ: Bueno, casi ...

GENO: Lo que pasa es que tú no quieres aceptar que Milagritos ha cambiado un montón desde que está en ese college de blanquitos ... (*Se oyen voces de la calle.*)

PEPE EL INDIO: (*De afuera.*) Rubén, Rubén, ¡no dejes que te maten los búfalos!

RUBÉN: (*De afuera.*) Don't worry, Chief, los tengo bien cercaos.

ANAMÚ: Ya está Pepe el Indio con su cantaleta. Horita entra a pedir chavos para el lunch. Lo tienes mal acostumbrado.

GENO: Es un pobre infeliz, Anamú. No tiene ni dónde dormir.

ANAMÚ: Es un borracho, mamá. El dinero que le das para comer va y se lo bebe en cerveza.

GENO: Por lo menos no se lo gasta en drogas.

RUBÉN: (*Entra* RUBÉN *vestido de pelotero, bate en mano. El uniforme es de colores muy escandalosos. En la espalda dice "Leones del Barrio".*) Buenas por aquí, doñas. ¿Qué se cuenta?

ANAMÚ: Qué tal, hijo . . .

GENO: (*Tapándose los ojos con el abanico.*) ¡Alabao, Rubén! ¡Ese uniforme da mareo!

RUBÉN: (*Se siente incómodo en el uniforme.*) Bueno . . . a caballo regalao no se le miran los dientes . . . José, el dueño del restaurant "La Bella Boricua" donó los uniformes. Yo le dije que se iban a burlar de nosotros, pero él dice que y que es para "confundir" al equipo contrario.

GENO: Será para confundirlos con náusea.

RUBÉN: Lo malo es que a "Los Bueyes del Bronx" no hay náusea que los maree. Pero, anyway, Doña Geno, para estar seguro deme acá una esencia de "Amansaguapo".

ANAMÚ: Ojalá que funcione. La última vez le dieron las nueve donas.

RUBÉN: (GENO *le da una botellita.*) Gracias, Doña Geno. Me lo apunta. (RUBÉN *la abre y la derrama sobre el bate.*)

GENO: No te preocupes, m'ijo. Voy a chequear la masa (*Señalando el uniforme.*) y a descansar mis ojos de esos colorines. (GENO *Sale.*)

RUBÉN: (*A* ANAMÚ.) ¿Masa, dijo? ¿Por casualidad será masa para hacer los famosos y únicos pasteles de Doña Geno Domínguez, la Emperatriz del Pastel Puertorriqueño? (*Se relame.*)

ANAMÚ: No te hagas la boca agua, Rubén. Los estoy haciendo yo. Mamá no se siente muy bien estos días. Además, son para la graduación de Milagros.

RUBÉN: ¿Ya se sabe la fecha?

ANAMÚ: No, estamos esperando su llamada. Quedó en avisarnos. Creo que es el otro fin de semana. Los vamos a congelar para tenerlos ready. Cincuenta pasteles no se hacen en un día.

RUBÉN: ¿Y Mila sabe que van a llevar pasteles a la graduación?

ANAMÚ: No, es una sorpresa.

RUBÉN: Una sorpresa, sí . . . ¿Quién lo iba a pensar, eh? Milagritos graduada en Business Administration. Lo digo, lo oigo y no lo creo.

GENO: (*Entra de atrás, caldero y cuchara en mano.*) Anamú, a esta masa no la salva ni un mila . . .

En ese momento se abre la puerta de la calle y entra MILLIE *cargada de paquetes y arrastrando una maleta.*

RUBÉN: ¡Mila!
ANAMÚ: ¡Milagros!
GENO: ¡Milagritos!
ANAMÚ: M'ija, pero ... (*Todos tratan de hablar a la vez, rodeándola y abrazándola.*)
RUBÉN: ¿Pero, qué tú hace aquì?
ANAMÚ: ... ¿y la graduación?
GENO: ¿Te pasa algo? ¿Por qué no llamastes?
ANAMÚ: ¿Cómo que no avisaste que venías?
RUBÉN: What happened?
GENO: ¿Te graduaste?
ANAMÚ: (*Confundida, ansiosa.*) ¿Y qué vamos a hacer con todos esos pasteles?
MILLIE: Cálmense, cálmense.
ANAMÚ: No me digas que no te graduaste. Después de tanto esfuerzo ...
MILLIE: Mami, sí me gradué. La graduación fue ayer. Mira la sortija ... Y aquí está el diploma.
GENO: ¡Ayer! ¿Cómo es posible? ¿Y por qué no avisaste? Aquí tu mamá y yo estábamos preparadas para arrancar para allá ...
ANAMÚ: Con cincuenta pasteles congelados ... Bueno ... todavía están sin congelar ...
RUBÉN: Milagritos .... .
MILLIE: (*Corrigiéndolo.*) Millie.
RUBÉN: Millie ... yo los iba a llevar en mi carro hasta allá arriba. Hasta un gabán me había comprado ... y una corbata seria ...
MILLIE: Mamá, abuela, Rubén ... lo siento muchísimo ... es que ... hubo problemas y adelantaron la fecha ... fue una ceremonia privada ... fue poquísima gente ... No hubo tiempo de avisar a nadie.
GENO: ¿Y es que en Nu Jamprish no hay teléfonos?
MILLIE: Es que con el nerviosismo y el apuro pensé que no quería que ustedes salieran corriendo para allá, así de un momento para otro. Además, no se perdieron nada del otro mundo. Fue aburridísimo todo.
ANAMÚ: ¡Nada del otro mundo! Mi hija se gradúa de la universidad y eso no es nada del otro mundo! Yo que estaba preparada para sentirme tan orgullosa.

MILLIE *se siente obviamente incómoda y avergonzada. No sabe qué decir.* DOÑA GENO *la mira con ojos llenos de pregun-*

tas. ANAMÚ *aparta la vista.* RUBÉN *se da cuenta del embarazo general. Tratando de salvar la situación.*

RUBÉN: Hey, people! Nos podemos sentir orgullosos aquí mismo. ¿No es verdad . . . Mila . . . digo, Millie? Vamos a celebrar la graduación aquí mismo. No tengo mi gabán nuevo, pero, ¡qué diablos, este uniforme es nuevo también! (*Saca el birrete que sobresale de una de las bolsas que Millie trae. Se lo pone a Millie*) A ver, el diploma . . . ¿dónde está? . . . Here it is! Man, are we proud or what! (*Agarra el diploma y lo enarbola como una espada.*) ¡A la carga, a hervir pasteles! *Salen. Apagón.*

Más tarde ese mismo día. Rubén y Millie están solos en la botánica.

RUBÉN: Entre tú y yo, Mila . . . Millie, los pasteles de tu mamá no son tan buenos como los de la abuela. Pero, fíjate, hoy me supieron de maravilla. Será por la ocasión . . . Tú casi ni los probastes.

MILLIE: Es que ya no como cerdo. Es un veneno para el cuerpo.

RUBÉN: No me vengas con esas. Si eso fuera verdad ya no quedaría un puertorriqueño vivo.

MILLIE: Tú te imaginas, ¡mamá y abuela llegando a mi graduación con cincuenta pasteles congelados!

RUBÉN: ¿Tú sabías que los iban a llevar?

MILLIE: No, pero me lo imaginaba. Yo las conozco. Cuando era chiquita íbamos a Orchard Beach en el subway. Todos los demás niños iban cargando sus juguetes, salvavidas, cubetas, palitas, toallas. Yo no. Yo iba cargando shopping bags llenos de pasteles y arroz con gandules. Creo que por eso no me gusta la playa.

RUBÉN: ¿Es por eso que no quisiste que fueran a la graduación?

MILLIE: (*Evasiva.*) ¿Por qué dices eso? Claro que no, fue porque . . . no hubo tiempo . . . no se dió la oportunidad . . . I thought I'd explained all that.

RUBÉN: Has cambiado mucho, Milagros . . .

MILLIE: Millie. No me gusta que me llamen Milagros.

RUBÉN: Es un nombre muy bonito, ¿qué tiene de malo?

MILLIE: Es que en la universidad . . . cada vez que les explicaba lo que quería decir se reían: »Miracles, what kind of a name is that!» decían.

RUBÉN: ¿Y tú le hacías caso a esa pendejá?

MILLIE: Tú no entiendes, Rubén. No fue fácil, ¿sabes? Llegar, sola a un lugar donde no conoces a nadie. Yo no había salido del Barrio como quien dice. Y caer allí, en New Hampshire, en una universidad donde casi todo el mundo era tan diferente a mí. It wasn't easy, believe me. Tuve que bregar con muchas cosas. Lo del nombre fue una de las más fáciles. Milagros en el Barrio puede ser común y corriente. Miracles in New Hampshire ... no way.

RUBÉN: Bueno, ya eso pasó. You're home now. Ahora estás aquí y tu familia está muy contenta– aunque no hayan podido ir a tu graduación.

MILLIE: ¿Nunca vas a olvidar eso?

RUBÉN: Es que tú no sabes lo entusiasmadas que estaban ... estábamos ...

MILLIE: Bueno, ya pasó. No quiero hablar más de eso. Lo que cuenta es el futuro.

RUBÉN: Eso sí. Doña Geno ya tiene sus años, y últimamente no se ha sentido bien ...

MILLIE: ¿Cómo puede ser? ¿Con tantos remedios y milagros al alcance de su mano? Yo la veo muy saludable. Ella es muy fuerte. Siempre lo dice: "A esta ceiba no hay rayo que la parta".

RUBÉN: Con tu preparación, serás una gran ayuda para tu abuela y tu mamá en la botánica.

MILLIE: Rubén, if you think I got a degree in business administration to run a botánica, you're out of your mind. Yo tengo otros planes.

RUBÉN: ¿Por ejemplo?

MILLIE: Por ejemplo: vice presidente del Chase Manhattan Bank—International Department.

RUBÉN: ¡Vaya, nena! Si vas a empezar por allá arriba, ¿por qué no presidente?

MILLIE: En un par de años. Ya verás. El caso es que ya tengo trabajo. Ellos fueron a reclutar al campus y me entrevistaron.

RUBÉN: ¿Tu familia sabe eso?

MILLIE: Mamá lo sabe, pero todavía no hemos encontrado el momento ... oportuno para decírselo a abuela.

RUBÉN: Good luck! Doña Geno piensa que te vas a quedar aquí. Yo también pensaba lo mismo.

MILLIE: Pues no, en cuanto empiece a trabajar me voy a mudar downtown. Quiero mi propio apartamento.

RUBÉN: Ahora sí que me convencí.

MILLIE: ¿De qué?

RUBÉN: De que se te cayó un tornillo por allá arriba. Hasta los gringos andan locos buscando apartamentos por aquí y tú, teniendo uno gratis aquí arriba, te vas a ir downtown a pagar por lo menos mil dólares de renta.

MILLIE: ¿Qué apartamento?

RUBÉN: El de Doña Fela. Se retira y se va para Puerto Rico. Tu abuela no lo va a rentar para dártelo. ¿No lo sabías?

MILLIE: No me ha dicho nada.

RUBÉN: La comunicación familiar aquí es de primera.

MILLIE: Será otra "sorpresa" que me tiene preparada ... Pero yo no puedo aceptar eso. A ella le hace falta la renta para el mortgage. Esta casa no está pagá todavía.

RUBÉN: Eso no es problema. Tú le pagas la misma renta que Doña Fela y ya está. Mira, el apartamento está bien chulo. Yo le puse pisos nuevos de madera, nada de carpeta. Se lo dije a Doña Geno, "a Milagros no le gusta ese linóleo del cinco y diez. She likes the real thing: parquet floors ... " Costó un fracatán, pero quedó por la maceta. Muchacha, ¡Doña Fela casi cambia de idea!

MILLIE: Rubén, yo no quiero vivir aquí. No voy a vivir aquí. Yo tengo mis propios planes. Quiero algo diferente. Quiero salir de todo esto, olvidarme del olor a plátano frito y a Agua de Florida. I hate this business. Siempre he querido escaparme de aquí, del incienso, del alcanfor, de los despojos y los santos, de la gente buscándole soluciones fáciles a los problemas de la vida, de mi abuela, manejándole la vida a todo el mundo, como una reina en su palacio de colesterol y pachulí. Yo habré nacido en el ghetto pero no tengo que vivir en él.

RUBÉN: Pero es que ... mira ... muchos profesionales hispanos se están mudando pa'cá otra vez ... ayudando a ...

MILLIE: No me interesa eso. No soy una social worker. Allá afuera hay un mundo más grande y yo quiero ser parte de él, para eso me he preparado. No quiero ser como tú, soñando con dar jonrones en el Yankee Stadium y conformarse con fly balls en el Parque Central. (RUBÉN *se quita la gorra y baja la cabeza. Pausa.*) I'm sorry, Rubén. Perdóname, pero es que desde que llegué me siento presionada por todos. Todo el mundo tiene planes para mí. Me tienen la vida planificada sin contar conmigo. It is MY life, you know.

RUBÉN: I know. Lo que pasa es que yo siempre he pensado que uno estudia y adelanta en la vida para superarse, para ser una MEJOR persona, no para convertirse en OTRA persona. (RUBÉN *sale tirando la puerta.*)

MILLIE: Rubén, wait ... !

GENO: (*Entrando de atrás.*) ¿Ya están peleando? Tú, siempre tan incordia. Espero que no le hayas salido con uno de tus desaires. Ese muchacho lleva esperando por ti toda una vida.

MILLIE: No sé por qué. Yo nunca le he dado motivo para que espere. Siempre ha sido y será un amigo de mi niñez, casi un hermano. Eso es todo.

GENO: (*Toma el shopping bag donde guarda sus cuentas y busca entre los papeles.*) Hasta un día. A todo le llega su momento.

MILLIE: ¿Qué buscas abuela?

GENO: Algo que te quiero enseñar. Una sorpresa.

MILLIE: (*A sí misma.*) No sé si resisto una sorpresa más. (MILLIE *coge varios de los pedazos de papeles que Geno ha sacado de la bolsa. Leyendo.*) "Paco: pasote, mejorana, tártago." (*Coge otro papel y lee.*) "Julia: bálsamo tranquilo, rompezaragüey." (*Coge otro papel y lee.*) "Dr. Martínez: sal pa'fuera, polvos voladores, collares, Eleguá de seis pulgadas ... " ¿Qué es esto, abuela?

GENO: Las cuentas.

MILLIE: Ya sé que son las cuentas. La última vez que estuve aquí te compré un file cabinet y un ledger, te organicé todos los papeles: cuentas a cobrar, cuentas a pagar ... pero veo que sigues con el mismo sistema.

GENO: Aquel sistema no resultó. La gente se asustaba cuando veían lo que me debían. Este sistema es mejor. Yo meto la mano en la bolsa, saco un papelito y les digo una cantidad que yo sé que pueden pagar. Me la pagan, hacen otra compra y se van felices.

MILLIE: Que dirían de este sistema de lotería en la Harvard Business School ... (MILLIE *coge otro papel. Es una carta. La lee.* GENO *sigue buscando. Entusiasmada.*) Creo que encontré lo que buscabas. ¡Esta es una buena sorpresa!

GENO: ¿Qué es eso?

MILLIE: Una carta del Ahabi Realty Company. Te quieren comprar el building. Te ofrecen un buen precio ... bueno, comparado con lo que te costó ...

GENO: No pienso vender la casa. Ni a ese precio, que es un robo, ni a ninguno.

MILLIE: Pero, ¿por qué abuela? Con ese dinero acabas de pagar el mortgage y te compras una casa en Guayama ...

GENO: ¿Qué voy a hacer yo en Guayama? Yo no estoy lista para el retiro, y además, allí tengo mucha competencia.

MILLIE: Bueno, pues en otro sitio. Al lado de la playa ... (MILLIE *dobla la carta y se la guarda en un bolsillo.*)

GENO: (*Saca otro shopping bag de debajo del mostrador y continúa buscando.*) No sé, Milagritos, después de cuarenta años aquí en este revolú de ciudad, creo que me aburriría allá sin nada que hacer. Por el momento, esta ceiba está aquí plantá. Además, no puedo dejarte sola a cargo de la botánica, así de pronto. Tienes mucho que aprender.

MILLIE: Abuela, de eso quería hablarte ...

GENO: ¡Ah, mírala aquí! (*Saca una revista de la bolsa.*) La tuve que esconder de tu mamá.

MILLIE: ¿Qué es?

GENO: (*Se sienta en su trono.*) Un reportaje sobre tu papá que salió en la revista "Réplica" ... deja que tú veas esto ... (*Pasa las páginas hasta que encuentra la que busca.*) Mira: "Comerciante del Año en Miami—Empresario cubano se hace millonario con línea de productos espirituales". (*Le da la revista a* MILLIE.) ¿Qué te parece? Un hombre que hace unos años no sabía la diferencia entre el mastuerzo y la yerba buena. Todo lo que sabe lo aprendió de mí, aquí en la Botánica La Ceiba, Lexington y 113, El Barrio. Nueva York. Todo. Y ahora yo soy una de sus clientes. Y con lo caro que vende ... (*Apunta a la revista.*) Mira lo gordo que está. Y ahora fuma tabacos ... Fíjate en la medalla de oro que lleva, es del tamaño de una alcapurria. Esa se la compró con tó' los chavos que le he pagado por el Aerosol Siete Potencias ...

MILLIE: ¡Abuela, no me gusta que hables así de papi!

GENO: Yo no se porqué lo defiendes tanto ... Tu mamá no lo sabe, pero yo hasta le hice un trabajito para que no se casara con él. Pero no resultó.

MILLIE: ¡Abuela, si no se hubieran casado yo no existiría!

GENO: Claro que sí. Anamú se hubiera casado con el otro novio que tenía, Henry Collazo. Un muchacho tan bueno ...

MILLIE y GENO: ... de las mejores familias de Guayama ...

GENO: Anjá. La única diferencia es que hubieras sido cien por ciento puertorriqueña. Pero tu mamá, tan romántica ella, siempre ha creído ciegamente en aquello de "un pájaro las dos alas".

MILLIE: Pero abuela, si yo no tengo nada de cubana.

GENO: Nada, excepto las ínfulas.

MILLIE: Nunca lo soportaste, lo sé. Pero es mi padre. Y la verdad es que era muy cariñoso y muy simpático. No puedes negar que nos divertíamos mucho con él. Nos daba alegría.

GENO: Sí, el problema era que le daba "alegría" a demasiada gente. Sobre todo a otras mujeres. Y a tu mamá se la quitó de un tirón. Desde que esa marielita se le metió por los ojos a Ramiro y se lo llevó para Miami, tu mamá no es sombra de lo que era. A veces se olvida hasta de peinarse. Y mira que le he hecho trabajos especiales. Hasta preparé un baño de despojo especialmente para ella. Mira, hasta lleva su nombre: (*Le muestra una botellita.*) "Anamú Despojo Bath» ... Hice riegos y sahumerios en su cuarto por un tubo y siete llaves. Pero se ha vuelto inmune a mis trabajos.

MILLIE: Ya se le pasará.

GENO: Van para ocho años, m'ija. A ver si ahora que tu estás aquí la sacas a pasear, la llevas a la peluquería. Ella es todavía una mujer joven y atractiva. Puede casarse otra vez. Hace tres años que no pasa de la calle 110. Ahora que te tenemos aquí con nosotras otra vez ...

MILLIE: Abuela ... escúchame, de eso quería hablarte ... yo ...

ANAMÚ: (*Entra* ANAMÚ *con los brazos llenos de sobres de manila.*) Mamá, ¿dónde te pongo este incienso Don Dinero?

GENO: Allí, en el lugar de siempre.

ANAMÚ: (*Mira detrás del mostrador.*) ¡Pero mamá, si aquí hay tres cajas llenas! Me dijiste que no quedaban. Yo ordené cuatro cajas más. Tenemos incienso hasta el Día del Juicio Final.

PEPE: (*Entrando de la calle.*) Doña Geno, nos están matando los búfalos.

GENO: Y como.

MILLIE: (*Aparte a* ANAMÚ.) ¿Mamá, quién es ese señor? ¿De qué habla?

ANAMÚ: Es un borracho medio loco que ahora duerme por ahí por los edificios abandonados.

PEPE: (A MILLIE.) Joven, tiene que proteger sus bufalitos. Sin ellos no somos nada. A mí me los mataron todos y ya ve, no soy nada. Pero no se preocupe, aquí usted está bien protegida, sí señora, sí, porque aquí Doña Geno tiene su ceiba y esa no hay quien se la tumbe, ¿verdad, Doña Geno?

GENO: No hay rayo que la parta, chief.

PEPE: Pero los búfalos, eso es otra historia . . .

MILLIE: Pero, ¿qué búfalos son esos?

PEPE: Joven, usted ve eso allá afuera . . . ¿Lo ve? Bueno, pues to' esto aquí estaba antes lleno de búfalos. Y esos búfalos eran to' pa' nosotros . . .

MILLIE: ¿Búfalos? ¿En El Barrio?

PEPE: Jé, ¡que si qué! Ahí, por ahí mismito andaban . . . todo eso . . . lleno de búfalos, corriendo pa'rriba y corriendo pa'bajo, levantando polvo con las patas. Pero llegaron los blanquitos y pum pum pum, los mataron a to' y nos quedamos sin na' . . . y antes éramos dueños de to' . . . de to'. ¿Verdad, Doña Geno? Ella sabe, ella sabe lo que yo digo, ¿verdad Doña Geno, verdad?

GENO: Verdad.

PEPE: Pero Doña Geno tiene su ceiba—y a esa no hay quien la tumbe—no hay rayo que la parta.

GENO: (DOÑA GENO *le da un dolar.*) Aquí tiene, chief. Vaya y tómese una sopa caliente.

PEPE: (PEPE *coge el dólar y trata de metérselo en un bolsillo que no encuentra.*) Gracias Doña Geno, gracias. (A MILLIE, *saliendo.*) Joven, no deje que le maten sus búfalos, no deje que le pase lo que a mí. Que no se le olvide, niña, que no se le olvide . . . (PEPE *sale.*)

MILLIE: Pero, ¿quién es ese hombre?

ANAMÚ: (*Va a contestar cuando ve la revista que* GENO *tiene en las manos.* GENO *trata de esconderla. Sumamente alterada.*) Pero, ¿qué hace eso aquí? ¡Yo quemé esa revista hace un mes! ¡Eché las cenizas en un coco y lo tiré del ferry de Staten Island!

GENO: ¡Ay, bendito, m'ija! ¿Por qué no me lo dijiste? Como no la encontré fui y compré otra. La tenía guardada para enseñársela a Millie. Sin saber, te eché a perder el fufú. Pero, no te preocupes, yo arreglo esto, tu verás. Le voy a hacer mi "contra-burundanga special" ahora mismo. (*Escoge esencias y yerbas que va poniendo sobre el mostrador.*)

MILLIE: Dejen a mi papá tranquilo. Acuérdate, abuela, que tu misma lo has dicho: "los cubanos tienen muy buenas relaciones con sus santos—tienen pala con los espíritus".

GENO: Sí, es verdad. Pero a esta ceiba . . . (*Se da en el pecho.*) no hay quien la tumbe . . . (GENO *hace un gesto de malestar.*)

ANAMÚ: Mamá, ¿qué te pasa?

GENO: Nada . . . parece que algo me cayó mal . . .

MILLIE: Seguro que fueron las morcillas, esos petardos de colesterol ... Tómate un Alka Seltzer ...

GENO: Qué Alka-Seltzer, ni qué nada ... Un buen cocimiento de ...

ANAMÚ: Eso mismo. Ven, mamá, que te lo voy a hacer ... Millie ... atiende la botánica un momento. (GENO y ANAMÚ *salen.*)

MILLIE: (*Saca la carta de Ahabi Realty del bolsillo. Va al teléfono y marca un número. En el teléfono.*) Hello, Ahabi Realty? Yes ... I'm calling for Mrs. Genoveva Domínguez. It is about Mr. Ahabi's letter. Yes ... We are interested in his offer to buy the building ... . 113th Street, that's the one. I'd like to make an appointment with Mr. Ahabi to discuss the matter ... Next Tuesday is okay ... thank you. (MILLIE *cuelga. Devuelve la carta al bolsillo.*)

CARMEN: (*Entra de la calle.*) Buenas tardes ... ¡Ay, pero si mira quién es! Milagrito, ¿cómo tú estás?

MILLIE: Muy bien gracias, Carmen.

CARMEN: ¿Qué tal quedó la graduación? Doña Geno y Anamú no hacían más que hablar de eso. Me imagino que estarían como dos pavos reales en esa graduación. (*Mira a su alrededor.*) ¿Y Doña Geno, por dónde anda?

MILLIE: Doña Geno está descansando.

CARMEN: ¿Descansando? ¡Ay, bendito, espero que no esté enferma!

MILLIE: Parece que tiene indigestión.

CARMEN: ¡Ay, la pobre! Le voy a encender una vela y a rezarle la oración que ella me dió cuando mi mamá se operó de la vesícula.

MILLIE: No es para tanto. Fueron las morcillas que se comió. Pero, gracias de todos modos.

CARMEN: No hay de que, m'ija. Doña Geno me ha ayudado mucho en momentos difíciles. Mira, ahora mismo necesito de sus consejos—pero bueno, vendré mañana ...

MILLIE: ¿Qué te pasa?

CARMEN: No sé. Nada me va bien. Quiero cambiar mi vida. Mi novio me dejó. Es el tercero este año. Necesito una receta espiritual, algún riego diferente, una limpieza nueva. ¿Qué tu crees?

MILLIE: Yo te aconsejaría que vayas a la escuela por la noche, aprendas inglés, te consigas otro trabajo. También cómprate ropa nueva. Y cámbiate el peinado. Eso siempre ayuda.

CARMEN: ¡Ay, pero es mucho trabajo! Yo no tengo tiempo para esas cosas. Ni dinero.

MILLIE: Cambiar de vida siempre cuesta.

CARMEN: (*Alicaída, decepcionada con los consejos.*) No sé. Necesito algo más. Mejor vengo mañana . . . cuando esté Doña Geno.

MILLIE: Bueno . . . mira, tal vez puedas ir haciendo algo mientras tanto. Aquí tengo un libro . . . (*Saca una libreta de detrás del mostrador.*) Vamos a ver . . . (*Ojea la libreta.*) A ver . . . recetas espirituales para la suerte . . . para el trabajo . . . para conseguir hombres . . . anjá, éste es . . . (*Lee en voz alta.*) "Se hierven siete ramitos de yerba buena, se le agrega miel, ron y el contenido del baño-despojo 'Suerte Rápida', un pedazo del . . . pantie que esté usando el día que realice este trabajo, se deja enfriar el agua y luego se coloca frente a la imagen de Yemayá, y se le enciende una vela amarilla. Se tiene una noche, y al otro día, moje con esa agua la suela de sus zapatos, y limpie la entrada de la casa con el resto, pronunciando estas palabras: 'Que por esta puerta entre el hombre que me haga feliz'. Hágalo tres viernes seguidos . . . "

CARMEN: ¡Ay, ésa creo que no fallará!

MILLIE: Espera, hay más . . . (*Pretende leer.*) "Vaya a la peluquería y cámbiese el peinado. Rece tres Padres Nuestros y cómprese un vestido nuevo— amarillo. Mejore su apariencia y su vida. Vaya a la escuela por la noche y aprenda inglés".

CARMEN: ¿Ahí dice eso? Deja ver . . . (*Trata de coger la libreta. Millie la retira.*)

MILLIE: No te lo puedo enseñar. Este es el libro secreto y sagrado de recetas de la abuela y ella no se lo enseña a nadie.

CARMEN: Bueno . . . me parece algo raro eso del final.

MILLIE: Es que son recetas modernas.

CARMEN: Ya decía yo. Está bien. Voy a probar. Gracias, Milagritos. Y ya sabes, estoy rezando por Doña Geno.

MILLIE: Bueno . . . gracias . . . y buena suerte.

CARMEN: Adiós, m'jita.

CARMEN *sale. Entra* ANAMÚ *cargando dos enormes figuras de santos. Una es de Santa Bárbara, la otra de San Lázaro. Las pone en uno de los estantes.*

MILLIE: ¿Y abuela?

ANAMÚ: (*Preocupada.*) Está echando una siesta

MILLIE: Qué bueno ...

ANAMÚ: Yo no le veo nada de bueno. A mi me huele mal.

MILLIE: ¿Por qué?

ANAMÚ: Tu abuela jamás en su vida ha dormido la siesta.

MILLIE: Pues ya era hora.

ANAMÚ: Nena, ponle las etiquetas con el precio a estos santos, por favor. Mira, están ahí ...

MILLIE: ¿A cómo son?

ANAMÚ: $79.95

MILLIE: ¿No están un poco caros?

ANAMÚ: Eso es casi lo que cuestan. (MILLIE *escribe las etiquetas y se las pega a la base de los santos.* ANAMÚ *la mira.*) Estoy preocupada por mamá.

MILLIE: Abuela es una mujer muy fuerte, pero tiene que tener cuidado con lo que come.

ANAMÚ: No estoy segura que sea indigestión ... Me preocupa, porque, tú sabes ... su corazón ... Ya no late al mismo ritmo que antes.

MILLIE: Es natural, a esa edad ya nada funciona igual que antes—a todos nos pasará ...

ANAMÚ: Ay, si ocurriera un milagro ...

MILLIE: Lo que abuela tiene que hacer es ir al médico y hacerse un buen chequeo.

ANAMÚ: No, lo que hace falta es un milagro ... que tú cambies de idea y no cojas ese trabajo en el banco y te quedes aquí con nosotras.

MILLIE: Mamá, no voy a cambiar de planes. Ya te lo he dicho de todas las maneras posibles. No hay que hablar más de eso. Yo empiezo a trabajar en el banco en dos semanas—and that's that.

ANAMÚ: Yo no sé cómo decírselo a mamá ... ¿Y si se enferma ... ?

MILLIE: Nada, vendemos la casa. Te mudas a Guayama. Allí está toda la familia. Ya hay alguien interesado en comprar el edificio.

ANAMÚ: Pero, qué voy a hacer yo, una mujer sola, sin marido ...

MILLIE: Aquí siempre nos la hemos arreglado muy bien sin hombres. Ellos han entrado y han salido de nuestras vidas. Eso es todo. Abuela desde que se quedó viuda tan joven, siempre se las arregló muy bien sola. Te crió a ti y me crió a mí—y cuando mi padre se largó ...

ANAMÚ: Eso sí ... nos las hemos arreglado solas, y ¡nunca hemos vivido del welfare! ¡Muy duro que trabajamos!

MILLIE: Pues debías entenderme mejor.

ANAMÚ: Si te entiendo, m'ijita, pero yo no soy como tú ... tengo miedo ... Mamá siempre ha sido como esa ceiba de la que tanto habla. Cobijándome en su sombra, protegiéndome de los rayos que manda la vida ...

MILLIE: Pero tú fuiste joven como yo. ¿Nunca quisiste ser tu propia ceiba?

ANAMÚ: Nunca se me ocurrió. Cuando conocí a tu padre, él también andaba en busca de protección y abrigo. Y aquí lo encontró ... Pero antes, sí. Cuando estaba en high school ... yo pensaba ... yo soñaba con— te vas a reír ... nunca se lo he contado a nadie— pero yo quería ser cantante.

MILLIE: ¡Mamá! ¡Tú, cantante! ¡Nunca me lo hubiera imaginado!

ANAMÚ: Estaba en el coro de la escuela. Todo el mundo me decía que tenía una voz tan linda ...

MILLIE: Pero ... si yo nunca te he oído cantar ...

ANAMÚ: Sí, me has oído.

MILLIE: ¿Cuándo?

ANAMÚ: Cuando eras una bebita.

MILLIE: Ah, eso no cuenta. Cántame algo ahora ...

ANAMÚ: ¿Aquí? ¡Estás loca! Para que mamá venga y ...

MILLIE: Anda, sí, un pedacito ... Ella no te va a oír.

ANAMÚ: No, no ...

MILLIE: Dale, mamá.

ANAMÚ: (ANAMÚ *canta. A mitad de la canción se oyen ruidos de la casa.* ANAMÚ *deja de cantar súbitamente. Entra* GENO.) Mamá, ¿qué haces aquí? Quedamos en que te ibas a quedar descansando ...

GENO: Ya descansaré bastante cuando me muera. No fue más que un mareo. Ahora tengo mucho que hacer. Tengo que enseñarle a Millie los remedios y las recetas ...

ANAMÚ y MILLIE *intercambian una mirada.* MILLIE *le hace señas a* ANAMÚ *que le hable a la abuela.* ANAMÚ *niega con la cabeza. Le hace señas a* MILLIE *que lo haga ella.* MILLIE *se niega.* ANAMÚ *le da un codazo. Mientras,* GENO *busca y trastea detrás del mostrador y en los anaqueles.*

MILLIE: Abuela ... tenemos que ... hablar sobre ... (*Suena el teléfono.* MILLIE *lo contesta rápidamente. La salvó la campana.*) ¿Hello? ... Sí, es la Botánica La Ceiba ...

Millie . . . Milagros . . . . Bien, gracias . . . No, la graduación fue ayer . . . . Sí . . . No . . . Un momento. (*Tapa el auricular con la mano.*) Abuela, es Gloria la peluquera. Quiere hablar contigo.

GENO: Pregúntale qué quiere.

MILLIE: (*En el teléfono.*) Abuela está ocupada en este momento. Quiere saber qué pasa . . . . (*Escucha.*) Anjá . . . anjá . . . Un momento. (*Tapa el teléfono. A Geno.*) Dice que anoche soñó con unos calzoncillos. Que qué quiere decir eso . . . Para mí es que necesita marido.

GENO: ¡Ay virgen! ¡Dile que venga para acá corriendo!

MILLIE: ¿Por qué?

GENO: Soñar con ropa interior significa infelicidad en el hogar y pérdida de dinero . . . pero no le digas eso. Dile que venga, y que juegue el 184.

MILLIE: (*En el teléfono*) Gloria, dice abuela que pase por aquí en cuanto pueda. Y que juegue el 184. Pero, mire, yo le recomendaría que se leyera a Freud . . . F-R-E-U-D . . . Sí, pero se pronuncia "froid" . . . "La interpretación de los sueños" . . . No, abuela no tiene ese libro aquí . . . No, en la "Enciclopedia de Walter" no lo explican. Bueno, dice que la falta de relaciones sexuales puede . . .

GENO: (*Arrancándole el teléfono de las manos a Millie. En el teléfono.*) Gloria, no le hagas caso. Pasa por aquí más tarde que te voy a dar un resguardo . . . Sí . . . Puedes hacer una limpieza . . . hoy es . . . sábado . . . bueno, pues coges agua fresca, siete perfumes distintos, siete monedas de a centavo, siete pétalos de una flor roja y el perfume Imán para la suerte . . . sí . . . y no te olvides, juega el 184 . . . Okay. Hasta luego. (*Cuelga. A* MILLIE.) ¿Qué tú haces? Gloria es una santa mujer y tu hablándole de relaciones sexuales . . . ¿Es que te estás burlando de mis clientas?

MILLIE: ¡Ay, abuela, si Gloria es peluquera!

GENO: ¿Y eso qué tiene que ver?

MILLIE: ¿Tú has oído las conversaciones en las peluquerías? ¡Las cosas que se hablan allí! Y no me estoy burlando. Estoy siendo realista y científica. Gloria tiene 40 años, nunca ha tenido un marido y sueña con calzoncillos. ¿Qué tú crees que eso significa? ¡Bellaquera del subconsciente! Qué otra cosa va a ser. ¡Estamos casi en el siglo 21 y tu todavía pretendes resolverle los problemas a la gente con yerbas, esencias y mumbo jumbo!

ANAMÚ: ¡Milagros, no le hables así a tu abuela!

GENO: Gracias a ese "mumbo jumbo" fuiste a la universidad. ¿Por qué te crees tú que te ganaste esa beca?

MILLIE: ¡Porque estudié, me quemé las pestañas para sacar buenas notas y porque era la "spic" de turno para llevarme la beca! No me hago ilusiones, abuela. Yo brego con la realidad.

GENO: ¡Muchas oraciones y muchas velas a los santos y mucha fe, FE, Milagros! Gracias a eso te ganaste la beca. Gracias a eso hemos sobrevivido. Esta ceiba nos ha dado mucha sombra. Y mejor que cambies de actitud, porque así vas a espantar a los clientes. ¿De qué te sirve toda tu ciencia si no entiendes a la gente? Una botánica no es un negocio, es un *servicio.*

MILLIE: ¡No voy a espantar a ningún cliente, porque yo no voy a hacerme cargo de esta botánica!

GENO: ¡Qué!

MILLIE: Ya yo tengo un trabajo en un banco, que es donde está el único "espíritu" que cuenta en este mundo: ¡el dinero!

ANAMÚ: Milagros, ¡basta ya! ¡Es un sacrilegio! ¡Estas son nuestras tradiciones . . . !

MILLIE: ¿Sacrilegio de qué, mamá? Tú nunca has creído en nada de esto, pero te dejaste atrapar por las "tradiciones" . . . ¡dejaste de cantar! ¡Estas son cosas del pasado que no tienen nada que ver con el presente! (MILLIE *extiende un brazo y, sin querer, tira al piso varias imágenes y frascos.*)

GENO: (*Llevándose las manos al pecho.*) ¡Santos y santas, espíritus y potencias, no la oigan, no la escuchen! ¡No hagan caso de lo que dice! ¡Ella sí cree! ¡Lo que pasa es que se le olvidó, pero cree . . . ! (GENO *cae derrumbada sobre el mostrador.* MILLIE y ANAMÚ *corren hacia ella.*)

ANAMÚ: ¡Mamá!

MILLIE: ¡Abuela!

GENO: La graduación . . . la graduación . . . (*Pierde el sentido.*)

MILLIE: Abuela . . .

Apagón.

SEGUNDO ACTO

Varios días más tarde. MILLIE *está sola en la botánica. De una bolsa de papel saca un croissant y un café en taza de cartón.*

Abre el café y bebe un sorbo. Entra PEPE EL INDIO *calladamente. La observa.*

PEPE: La ceiba se está tambaleando, ¿verdad, niña?
MILLIE: (*Sobresaltada.*) ¡Me asustó! No lo vi entrar ...
PEPE: Yo me acuerdo cuando vi el primer búfalo caer muerto a mis pies ...
MILLIE: No tengo dinero que darle. No se ha vendido nada hoy.
PEPE: No vine a buscar dinero, niña. Vine a preguntar por Doña Geno.
MILLIE: Sigue igual. Pero hoy le van a cambiar el tratamiento. Yo creo que se va a mejorar pronto ...
PEPE: Ah, eso es importante, que usted *crea* que se va a mejorar ... (*Saca una botella de ron y bebe.*) Sí, hay que creer, aunque sea difícil. Mire, cuando empezaron a matarme los búfalos me quedé sin nada en qué creer ... ahora ... (*Levanta la botella, toma otro trago. Se limpia la boca con la mano.*) Pa' mi es muy tarde ... Lo primero que hay que hacer es no dejar que le maten los búfalos ... Acuérdese de eso, niña ... acuérdese.

MILLIE *le da la espalda para buscar su cartera. Saca un dólar. Cuando se voltea, billete en mano,* PEPE EL INDIO *ya no está.* MILLIE *mira a su alrededor, buscándolo. FOCO sobre una estatua de indio.* MILLIE *se queda observándolo.*

RUBÉN: (*Entra* RUBÉN.) Hola.
MILLIE: Hola.
RUBÉN: Me encontré con Anamú en el subway. Me contó que llamaron del hospital y que iba a firmar unos papeles ...
MILLIE: Sí, a abuela le van a cambiar el tratamiento, y necesitan autorización ...
RUBÉN: ¿Qué tú crees?
MILLIE: No sé, Rubén, no sé. No sé qué va a pasar. Estoy muy confundida ...
RUBÉN: There's nothing to be confused about ...
MILLIE: A veces me siento culpable de lo que pasó, por decirle las cosas a mi abuela, así de cantazo. Y por lo de la graduación ... lo último que dijo fue, "la graduación" ... casi sonó como una acusación ... (*Para sí.*) Si ella supiera ...
RUBÉN: Te estás imaginando cosas, Millie. Doña Geno no ...
MILLIE: Otras veces pienso que mi abuela está tratando de crear su propio milagro, estando a punto de morirse para hacer que yo cambie de planes y me quede a cargo de la botánica ...

RUBÉN: Milagros, ¿cómo puedes pensar eso?
MILLIE: Tú no conoces a mi abuela como yo.
RUBÉN: Pero éste no es el momento de pensar esas cosas.
MILLIE: ¿Y cuál es el momento?
RUBÉN: Si quieres empezar otra pelea, I'm not in the mood. Anyway, vine a otra cosa.
MILLIE: No es una pelea, es una discusión. Me siento que estoy en el medio de una conspiración, que soy víctima de una manipulación emocional y sicológica ... Hasta me parece que los santos me miran mal. ¡Y ese indio parece que me va a tirar el hacha!
RUBÉN: ¿Pepe?
MILLIE: No. Ese. (*Señala la estatua de un indio de hacha en mano.*)
RUBÉN: Millie, no sé de que conspiración hablas. Yo lo que creo es que tú ...
MILLIE: No logro hacerles entender que yo no soy parte de esto. Estas imágenes, estas creencias, han sido parte del equipaje de otras generaciones ... del Africa al Caribe, del Caribe a Nueva York ... pero yo soy de aquí, yo nací aquí. Esto no es parte de mi equipaje ... you know what I mean. Tú naciste aquí también. ¿Tú entiendes lo que yo digo?
RUBÉN: No sé ... Yo veo las cosas de otra manera ... Mira, no sé si te lo puedo explicar, si tengo las palabras. Yo no fui a una universidad tan fancy como la tuya. Yo nada más me gradué de Hostos College ... en el Bronx.
MILLIE: ¿Tú también me echas en cara mi educación?
RUBÉN: (*Tentativo, escogiendo cuidadosamente las palabras.*) No, no es eso ... no sé ... ¿Qué quiere decir "ser de aquí"? ... Pues ... pa' mi "ser de aquí" es ... pues ... es mango y strawberries ... alcapurrias y pretzels ... Yemayá y los Yankees ... Yo no veo la diferencia. What's the big deal? Eso es lo que somos: brunch y burundanga, quiche y arroz con habichuelas, Chase Manhattan y la bolita ... Todo depende de como empaques tu equipaje. Pero todo es parte de él. Todo es la misma cosa .... You see, I decide what it means to be from here, porque allá afuera hay muchos que piensan que aunque hayas nacido aquí y te cambies el nombre a Joe o Millie, they think you're not from here anyway. De aquí, de allá ... que sé yo ... No hay por qué dejarlo todo atrás ... no hay que dejar que nos maten los búfalos ...

MILLIE: (*Pausa. Trata de absorber la explicación de Rubén.*) Dale con los búfalos . . .

RUBÉN: Ahí donde tú ves, Pepe el Indio es un hombre muy leído. El dice eso porque leyó que los indios americanos perdieron no sólo sus tierras, sino también su cultura e identidad cuando el hombre blanco les mató los bufalos.

MILLIE: Pero si no somos indios . . .

RUBÉN: El dice que cuando dejamos que nos maten las cosas que más nos importan, no somos más que tribus encerradas en reservaciones.

MILLIE: (*Mirándolo inquisitivamente.*) Todo eso no lo aprendiste en Hostos, ¿eh?

RUBÉN: Pues, sí. (*Pausa silenciosa.*)

MILLIE: Rubén . . .

RUBÉN: ¿Sí?

MILLIE: Gracias.

RUBÉN: ¿Por qué?

MILLIE: Por . . . no sé, por hablarme así. Ha sido un descanso no tener que estar a la defensiva . . .

RUBÉN: (*Le toma una mano.*) You don't have to be.

MILLIE: (*Retirando la mano.*) Maybe.

RUBÉN: (*Cambiando el tema.*) Bueno . . . ¿por qué no vienes al meeting?

MILLIE: ¿Qué meeting?

RUBÉN: ¡Pero que sonso, si no te lo he dicho! Es una reunión de vecinos que organizamos donde yo trabajo. Pensé que te haría bien poner tu mente en otra cosa.

MILLIE: ¿Para qué es la reunión?

RUBÉN: Hay unos especuladores que quieren comprar los buildings por aquí . . . ofreciendo una miseria. Lo que no dicen es los planes que tienen. En cuanto los compran botan a los inquilinos. Gentrification is coming to El Barrio, Mila.

MILLIE: Rubén, ahora no tengo mi cabeza para eso. La venta hay que pensarla bien. Hay que hacer un buen negocio. Pero ahora no estoy para eso. Tengo que pensar.

RUBÉN: ¿Quieres decir que también le quieren comprar a Doña Geno? Tú no estás pensando vender . . .

MILLIE: Sí. Hablé con Ahabi, pero abuela no quiere ni hablar de eso. Ese es un asunto que tengo que resolver luego. Tengo muchas cosas que resolver.

RUBÉN: ¿Que si cómo?

MILLIE: Creo que voy a cerrar ya. Casi no ha venido nadie. Todo el mundo quiere los consejos de Doña Geno. No sé qué

hago aquí, yo no sirvo para este negocio.
RUBÉN: Es que esto no se aprende de un día para otro. Recuerda lo que decía ... dice ... Doña Geno ...
RUBÉN y MILLIE: "Hay que aprender a freír despacio".
RUBÉN: Hasta mañana, Milagros. Si me necesitas ... llámame.
MILLIE: Hasta mañana.

RUBÉN *sale.* MILLIE *cierra la puerta detrás de él. Se queda pensativa unos segundos. Apaga algunas luces. Recoge algunos papeles que hay sobre el mostrador. Coge el croissant y le da una mordida. No sabe donde poner los papeles. Mira a su alrededor, ve el shopping-archivo de la abuela. Se sonríe y echa los papeles dentro de la bolsa. Le da otra mordida al croissant. Mira a su alrededor. Se detiene frente al grabado de la ceiba. Se queda pensativa.*

GENO: (*Voice over.*) ... cuando el diluvio universal la ceiba fue el único árbol que las aguas no cubrieron. Todos los animales y la gente que se refugiaron bajo la ceiba lograron sobrevivir y así fue que se volvió a poblar el planeta .... Al pie de la ceiba están enterrados los bilongos y los ebbós. Nunca debes cruzar su sombra sin pedir permiso. La ceiba es nuestra yaya, Milagritos, la madre de los espíritus. En africano se llama *Irokó* y también se llama *nkunia casa sami*, y se llama *mamá Ungundu* y se llama *Iggi-Olorún* y se llama ...
MILLIE: (*Bajito.*) Yaya ... (MILLIE *mira a su alrededor. Como la que no quiere la cosa, con disimulo enciende una vela. Cuando va a rallar el fósforo, algo le hace detenerse. Suelta los fósforos. Coge una botella de Agua de Florida y echa unas gotitas al piso. Echa unas gotas más. Luego esparce todo el contenido de la botella por la botánica.*) Maybe I'm not doing it right, but it can't hurt. (*Coge una botella de aerosol de la buena suerte y echa spray al aire. Mira las imágenes de los santos, trata de decir algo, pero no le sale. Se dirige a una imágen de Santa Bárbara.*) Excuse me ... I ... I've forgotten how to do this ... I don't know what to say, but ... Saint Barbara ... I'll go straight to the point: please make my granma well. (*Luz sobre la imágen de* SANTA BÁRBARA.)
SANTA BÁRBARA: (*Voice over. Con acento cubano.*) No falla. Nada más que se acuerdan de mí cuando truena. Y mira, chiquitica, yo no spika inglis.
MILLIE: Perdón. No me di cuenta. Rogaba por mi abuela, para que se salve.

SANTA BÁRBARA: (*Voice over.*) M'ija, el que está a cargo de los enfermos es San Lázaro. El sí que es bilingüe.

MILLIE: Es verdad. No me acordaba. Gracias. (*Se para frente a San Lázaro. Luz en la imagen.*) No me acuerdo ... but wait ... a lo mejor me acuerdo ... Babalú-ayé, ese eres tú ... dueño del universo, salvador de todas las dolencias, dios de los que sufren enfermedades ... Taíta cañeñe ... Pan viejo te pondré detrás de la puerta ... Se me olvidó que me olvidé ... de tus dos perros y tus muletas ... guía y fe de los enfermos ... De ofrenda se te pone oro, de eso sí me acuerdo ... oro a tus pies y pan viejo detrás de la puerta ... (*Se quita el anillo de graduación y lo pone a los pies de la estatua.*) Que se ponga bien ya, San Lázaro. And make it quick, santo, please make it quick ...

GENO: (*Voice over.*) Milagritos, eres muy impaciente. En la vida hay que aprender a freír despacio, si no, tu vida será una fuente de tostones achicharrados ...

MILLIE: ¡Pero no hay tiempo, Yaya, no hay tiempo! ¡Santos, no hay tiempo!

SAN LÁZARO: (*Voice over.*) Hija, sólo soy un pobre viejo enfermo que hace milagros. Se hace lo que se puede, hija. We win one, we lose one. But we keep trying.

MILLIE: Win this one, will you. Win this one, please!

SAN LÁZARO: (*Voice over.*) Vamos a ver lo que se puede hacer, hija. Y a cambio, ¿qué me prometes?

MILLIE: ¿Prometer? No sé qué puedo prometer .... ¡Ah, ya sé! ¡Tú también eres parte de la conspiración! Si piensas que voy a dejar mi trabajo en el banco y quedarme aquí, olvídalo. Ese diploma me costó lágrimas y sangre y no lo voy a desperdiciar. Además, no te pido que lo hagas por mí, sino por ella ... Yaya ... abuela. Ella les ha prometido todo. Y les ha dedicado toda su vida.

SAN LÁZARO: (*Voice over.*) Tienes que prometer algo. Business is business.

MILLIE: What do you mean »business is business»? Esto no es un negocio—we are talking miracles here ... Okay?

SAN LÁZARO: (*Voice over.*) ¿Y tú crees que los milagros no cuestan?

MILLIE: I see, you want to play hardball, don't you? That's fine with me. I can play too. Look, I won't make you a promise, but I'll make you a deal—an offer you can't refuse.

SAN LÁZARO: (*Voice over.*) I'm listening.

MILLIE: (*Acercándose al santo.*) Yo, Milagros Castillo ... I, Miracles Castle ... have I got a deal for you!

Apagón

Hay un cambio de escenografía.

En la oscuridad se oyen martillazos, muebles que se mueven de un lado a otro, comentarios de RUBÉN, PEPE EL INDIO, MILLIE y ANAMÚ. *Puede tener una iluminación irreal o empezar medio a oscuras y las luces pueden ir subiendo poco a poco. Entre las cosas que suceden vemos a* RUBÉN *encaramado en una escalera colgando un letrero sobre el dibujo de la ceiba. El letrero dice: "Ceiba Tree Herbs and Candles Boutique".* MILLIE *coloca una calculadora electrónica sobre el mostrador.* PEPE y AMAMÚ *empujan un archivo de metal y lo colocan detrás del mostrador.* MILLIE *recoge los regueros y sacude el polvo, siempre chequeando lo que hacen los demás y dando órdenes. Cuando han terminado, todos se paran a contemplar lo que han hecho. Excepto* MILLIE, *nadie luce muy entusiasmado.* MILLIE *va y quita el trono de* DOÑA GENO *de debajo de la ceiba y lo pone hacia un lado. Vuelve a contemplar su obra con satisfacción.*

MILLIE: (*A los demás.*) ¿Qué les parece?

Apagón

Dos meses más tarde. Al subir las luces de nuevo, la botánica está vacía. Entra DOÑA GENO *de la casa con unas botellas de Despojo Bath en las manos. Las coloca en uno de los estantes. Ve la silla fuera de sitio. La coge y la vuelve a poner debajo de la ceiba. Entra* LUISA.

LUISA: ¡Doña Geno, no sabe la alegría que me da verla!

GENO: ¡Luisa, muchacha, tanto tiempo! (*Se abrazan.*)

LUISA: Ay, Doña Geno, ¡no sabe cómo recé por usted! Creíamos que se nos iba.

GENO: Qué va, m'ija. A esta ceiba no hay rayo que la parta.

LUISA: Se ve muy bien. ¿Cómo se siente?

GENO: De quince. Aquí hay Doña Geno para rato.

LUISA: (*Mirando a su alrededor.*) Y mire para allá, esta botánica está hecha un "boutique" ...

GENO: (*Disimulando su disgusto por los cambios.*) Cosas de mi nieta ... Pero, cuéntame de ti. ¿Cómo te van las cosas?

LUISA: ¿Vio como se me ha puesto el pelo Doña Geno? Esa sábila que me recomendó es una maravilla. Quiero llevarme un par de botellas más.

GENO: ¿Y Arturo, entró en cintura?

LUISA: Con él no tuvo ningún efecto la sábila. Se la di en cucharadas, en cápsulas, se la eché en el café, se la restregué por la cara ... y otras partes del cuerpo ... pero nada.

GENO: Puedo recomendarte otra cosa ... o si quieres te hago una cita con el babalao de Paterson ...

LUISA: Ay, ya no sé si vale la pena ... me estoy cansando un poco.

GENO: No te des por vencida, mijita ... mira, ¿por qué no pruebas las velas? ... Enciendes seis velas, una blanca, dos velas astrales, una roja —con unas gotitas de Aceite Fuego de Amor, una amarilla y una púrpura ... entonces haces esto que te voy a apuntar en este papelito ... (*Arranca un pedazo de papel de estraza de una bolsa —se da cuenta de lo que hace.*) Ay, si Milagritos me ve ... (*Bota el papel y saca una libreta grande y hace anotaciones y diagramas.*) Las mueves así por nueve días y nueve noches ... (*Arranca la hoja y se la entrega.*)

LUISA: (*Sin mucho entusiasmo.*) Bueno, no pierdo nada con probar ... deme las velas ...

LUISA: (*Entra* ANAMÚ *muy peinada y arreglada.*) ¡Anamú, te ves preciosa! ¿Qué te has hecho?

ANAMÚ: Nada. Milagritos me arregló el pelo. Eso es todo.

GENO: ¿A dónde vas tan emperifollada?

ANAMÚ: No sé.

GENO: ¿Cómo va a ser?

ANAMÚ: Millie quiere que vaya a una exposición de cosméticos naturales en el Coliseum —a ver si veo algo que podamos vender aquí en la botánica ...

GENO: A mí no me dijo nada de eso ...

ANAMÚ: Bueno ... me voy ... ni me acuerdo cómo llegar allá ...

LUISA: ¡Ay, yo te digo! Me conozco Nueva York de rabo a cabo. Estoy hecha una verdadera neoyorquina. Ya llevo aquí tres años.

ANAMÚ: (*Echándole una mirada.*) No te preocupes. Millie me dió un mapa.

GENO: De todas maneras, voy a encender una vela para que no te pierdas en el subway.

ANAMÚ: Gracias, mamá. Hasta luego. (ANAMÚ *sale hacia la calle.*)

LUISA: Anamú parece otra persona. Es increíble los cambios que se ven aquí, Doña Geno.

GENO: (*Sin mucho entusiasmo.*) Sí, desde que llegué del hospital las cosas van muy bien. Gracias a Dios, los santos y los espíritus.

LUISA: Me alegro mucho, Doña Geno. Usted se lo merece. Y ahora que Milagritos se mudó al apartamento de arriba, más contenta estará todavía.

GENO: Ella quería mudarse downtown, pero cuando vió las rentas que están pidiendo por un closesito, cogió pa' cá arriba a las millas de chaflán.

LUISA: Me imagino. ¿Ya es vice presidenta del banco?

GENO: Todavía ... pero está muy contenta con lo que hace —así dice.

LUISA: No sabe cuanto me alegro. Bueno, Doña Geno, me voy. ¿Cuánto le debo?

GENO: Son cinco pesos, m'ija.

LUISA: No, no. Cuánto le debo en total ... ¿Se acuerda el número que me dijo que jugara antes de irse al hospital? Me pegué. Así que le voy a pagar todo.

GENO: Qué bueno que puse una. Últimamente me estaban fallando los números. (*abre la gaveta, busca entre los folders y saca una hoja.*) Aquí está ... a ver ... son ... dame treinta pesos y estamos en paz.

LUISA: No, no, dígame lo que le debo de verdad.

GENO: (*Trata de sumar en la calculadora que está en el mostrador.*) Bueno ... pues son ... ¡ay, las cuentas no me salen en ese aparato! ... (*Coge papel y lápiz, saca cuenta.*) Cuatro y ocho, doce, llevo una siete y seis más ... Okay, son $63.60.

LUISA: ¿Está segura que no es más?

GENO: No, es eso nada más ...

LUISA: Okay ... (*Le paga.*) Aquí tiene, Doña Geno. Y gracias por todo. Hasta luego.

GENO: Aquí están tus velas. Hasta luego, m'ija. Que Dios te bendiga. (GENO *guarda el folder de nuevo en el archivo. Recoge otros papeles regados y los archiva. Coge un sacudidor de polvo y se lo pasa a los anaqueles. Arregla la mercancía. Sacude las imágenes. Mueve la estatua de San Lázaro para sacudir el estante. Se encuentra con la sortija de Millie. La mira extrañada, mira al santo interrogadoramente.*)

MILLIE: (*Entrando* MILLIE. *Se da cuenta que la abuela encontró la sortija.*) Hola, abuela. (*La besa.*)

GENO: Dios te bendiga, m'ijita. (*Pausa silenciosa.* GENO *mira la sortija, mira a* MILLIE. *Le enseña la sortija.*) Mira lo que me encontré.

MILLIE: No se me había perdido.

GENO: Entonces, ¿la dejaste de ofrenda? ¿Y el pan? ¿Pusiste pan viejo detrás de la puerta?

MILLIE: Más o menos ... dejé la mitad de un croissant.

GENO: ¿Crusán?

MILLIE: Es un pan. Francés.

GENO: ¿De Francia?

MILLIE: Sí ... no ... lo compré en la 96 ...

GENO: Ah, bueno ... entonces, esto quiere decir que hiciste una promesa.

MILLIE: (*Le quita la sortija de la mano a Geno. La pone detrás del santo.*) Nada de eso. Hice un trato. I made a deal with the santos.

GENO: ¿Un deal? M'ijita, con los santos no se negocea. Tú le das y ellos te dan.

MILLIE: Eso es un trato, isn't it, abuela?

GENO: No, no es lo mismo. ¿Quieres decir que si el santo no te cumple, lo llevas a la corte? ¿Le das un disposses?

MILLIE: No había pensado en eso.

GENO: Bueno, y ese trato, ¿Fue por mi?

MILLIE: Sí.

GENO: ¿Y para ti?

MILLIE: Para mi lo consigo yo con mis esfuerzos, con mis conocimientos y disciplina.

GENO: Mi niña, la vida no se puede vivir como un "business plan"

MILLIE: Abuela, tampoco se puede vivir de "milagros". (*Saca una botella de píldoras de la cartera. Se traga una.*)

GENO: ¿Qué te pasa? ¿Estás enferma?

MILLIE: Nada. Me duele un poco la cabeza.

GENO: Te voy a hacer un cocimiento de ...

MILLIE: Abuela, no quiero cocimientos. Con esta pastilla se me va a quitar ... (*Se da un leve masaje en las sienes.*)

GENO: Las yerbas son más saludables que esas cosas de botellas. Las yerbas son regalos de la Madre Natura. Mira, cuando el diluvio universal ...

MILLIE: Abuela, no estoy para historias.

GENO: Ese es el problema. Hoy en día nadie quiere saber nada de historias. Los jóvenes no quieren saber nada de las yerbas, ni de los remedios ... (*Se sienta en su trono debajo de la ceiba.*) Pero ya se darán cuenta cuando les falte. Porque al paso que vamos, la Madre Natura no dura mucho ... con tanto veneno que echan al aire y a los ríos y al mar.

MILLIE: Cantaleta time.

GENO: Cantaleta time, sí. ¿Tú te crees que porque ordenaste un poco la botánica y pusiste ese letrerito ahí y metiste los papeles en un archivo estás pagando la promesa que le hiciste a los santos?

MILLIE: Yo no hice ninguna promesa. I made a deal. Si tú te curabas yo iba a contribuir a que la botánica funcionara con más eficiencia y ...

GENO: Eso no es así. Uno no puede acordarse de Santa Bárbara nada más que cuando truena ...

MILLIE: (*Para sí.*) That's what she said.

GENO: ¿Qué?

MILLIE: Nada, nada ... (*Pausa.*) Si no te parece suficiente lo que he hecho ... puedo hacer más. Podemos cambiar la estantería, el color de la pared ... tu dirás ...

GENO: Es que nada de eso es lo que yo esperaba ...

MILLIE: ¿Y qué esperabas, abuela?

GENO: Yo esperaba enseñarte los secretos y los misterios, las maravillas de las plantas, las viejas historias y los ritos ... para que no se pierdan ... para que tus hijos y tus nietos las aprendan de ti como yo las aprendí de mi mamá, y ella de mi abuela, y mi abuela de su mamá y ella de su abuela y ...

MILLIE: Vivimos en otros tiempos, abuela. Mi mundo no es el tuyo. Esto no es Guayama, ni Africa. Este tipo de cosa no tiene futuro. Hoy en día ...

GENO: Claro que no tiene futuro si la gente joven no lo aprende ... si no hay continuidad, si no se preservan los secretos y los misterios, si no se entierran las cosas valiosas al pie de la ceiba ... (*Enciende una vela.*)

MILLIE: Abuela, pides demasiado de mí ... Yo tengo que vivir en el mundo allá afuera —y quiero triunfar ... estas cosas, estas ... no son más que ... a veces hay que renunciar ... (*Casi sin darse cuenta, trata de apagar la vela con la palma de la mano. La vela no se apaga.* MILLIE *se mira la palma de la mano.*)

GENO: Y tú has decidido renunciar ... yo no sé que te hicieron en esa universidad, Milagritos, pero cambiaste. Eso de no invitarnos a la graduación ... no sabes lo que me dolió ... nunca lo entenderé ...

MILLIE: (*Titubea brevemente, pero al fin se decide.*) La graduación ... no las invité porque no tenía nada que celebrar. Ése solo fue el día que me entregaron un diploma ... Mi verdadera "graduación" fue mucho antes, abuela ... el primer año de college. Esa fue mi prueba de fuego, abuela. (*Se mira la palma de la mano.*) Yo llegué allí a conquistar el mundo, a aprenderlo todo. Pero enseguida empezaron las pequeñas crueldades —burlas sobre mi ropa, sobre mi acento, sobre la música que me gustaba ... sobre mi nombre ... "Miracles, what kind of a name is that?" ... Yo no quería ser diferente, yo quería ser como las demás. Y me cambié el nombre a Millie y escondí mis discos de salsa. Y escondí los resguardos y los collares y los despojos que tú me enviabas —tus "survival kits". Un día mi compañera de cuarto encontró en el fondo del closet la caja donde yo había escondido todo aquello. La encontró, y no me dijo nada. Pero se lo contó a media escuela ... "Miracles Castillo, from El Barrio, is a witch —esa spik practica la brujería. ¿A que no saben lo que tiene escondido en el closet?" Pidió que la cambiaran de habitación. Unos días antes yo había solicitado a una de las sororidades. Y me habían aceptado. El día de la iniciación decidieron jugarme una broma. Me llevaron al bosque, de noche ... me vistieron con una toga, me hicieron caminar descalza sobre los pine cones, me amarrarona uno de los pinos ... a mis pies pusieron un montón de tissue paper —rojo. Parecía una hoguera. Encendieron velas. Me vaciaron encima una botella de ron. Una de ellas golpeaba un pequeño tamborcito de juguete. Las demás bailaron a mi alrededor, como una danza india y ... yo sé que fue un accidente, pero ... a una de ellas se le cayó la vela ... y aquella hoguera de papel se convirtió en una hoguera de verdad. En la confusión, en lo que me desamarraban, mis pies, empapados de ron ... My feet got burned, abuela! (GENO *la abraza.*) But I didn't quit, I didn't quit. Porque eso es lo que quieren, que nos demos por vencidos. Pero, gané. Y me gradué. Summa Cum Laude.

GENO: (*Meciéndola en sus brazos. Sin reproche.*) Pero, m'ijita, de que sirve ganar si dejas de ser quien eres ...

MILLIE: ¿Y quiénes somos, abuela? ¿Quiénes somos?

Apagón gradual. Por unos segundos sólo se ve la luz de la vela y los perfiles de MILLIE, GENO y SANTA BÁRBARA. *Apagón total.*

Varios días más tarde. Al subir las luces de nuevo, la botánica está vacía. De afuera se oyen las voces de PEPE EL INDIO, RUBÉN *y* MILLIE.

PEPE: ¡Rubén, Rubén, agárralo bien! ¡Que no se te escape, muchacho!

RUBÉN: Chief, lo tengo bien agarrado por aquí. Cuidado no tropieces allí.

PEPE: Esto pesa más que un búfalo muerto.

MILLIE: Esperen, esperen ... cuidado no se les caiga ... (RUBÉN y PEPE *entran cargando una caja enorme. Detrás entra* MILLIE *empujando una mesita con ruedas. Entre todos abren la caja.* RUBÉN *saca el monitor de una computadora.* MILLIE *saca el teclado,* PEPE *saca el disc drive, luego la impresora. Lo ponen todo sobre la mesa con ruedas.*)

GENO: (*Entra* GENO *de la casa.*) ¿Y esto qué es?

MILLIE: Una sorpresa, abuela. ¡Taíta!

GENO: (*Dándole la vuelta a la mesa. Intrigada.*) Muy bonito, pero, ¿qué es?

MILLIE: It's a computer, abuela! Una computadora.

GENO: ¿Y qué voy a hacer yo con eso?

MILLIE: Lo mismo que has hecho siempre, pero mejor. Y más rápido.

GENO: ¿Y tú crees que a mi edad yo voy a aprender a manejar ese coso?

MILLIE: Yo te voy a enseñar, abuela. Todos los días cuando salga del trabajo, vengo a darte clases. Y a mamá también.

ANAMÚ: (*Entra* ANAMÚ.) ¿Mamá qué? ¿Qué te traes entre manos ahora?

GENO: Anamú, mira con lo que se ha aparecido esta muchacha, una competidora.

MILLIE: Computadora, abuela.

ANAMÚ: ¿De dónde salió eso?

MILLIE: En el banco cambiaron el sistema a uno más moderno y vendieron éstas a los empleados baratísimas.

GENO: ¿Y para qué sirve esto?

MILLIE: Esto tiene una memoria, y todo lo que tú le enseñes, ella se acuerda.

GENO: Para eso no hace falta un aparato. Yo me acuerdo de todo.

MILLIE: Pero con esto, todos tenemos acceso a la información.

GENO: ¿Y cómo funciona?

MILLIE: Bueno, primero hay que ponerle adentro la información. En estos discos se graban las cosas, ¿ves? Aquí vamos a poner todas las yerbas, los remedios, las oraciones, los sueños, los riegos, los sahumerios, las limpiezas de la semana. En otro vamos a poner el inventario, así siempre sabrás qué cantidades te quedan de cada producto, el costo, etc. Después aprietas estas teclas, y aquí por la pantalla sale la información que quieres. Y si quieres imprimirlo, aprietas esta otra, y ¡rácata! sale por allá en papel.

ANAMÚ: ¿Y no es peligrosa?

MILLIE: No, mamá, no muerde.

PEPE: Doña Geno, ¿qué usted cree? Esto es otro invento de los blanquitos ... Hay que tener cuidado. Tiene que tener cuidado con los búfalos, Doña Geno ...

GENO: No sé, Chief. No sé que pensarán los santos y los espíritus de todo esto.

MILLIE: Abuela, de eso no te preocupes. It is okay with them, I assure you. (*Le da una palmadita a la computadora.*) Aquí, en esta memoria vamos a enterrar todo los secretos —como si fuera al pie de la ceiba. ¿Qué te parece?

GENO: Ay, nena, yo no se ... ¿Tú crees que una vieja como yo va a poder aprender estos aparatos?

RUBÉN: ¡Déjese de eso, Doña Geno!

MILLIE: Sí, vas a poder. Toma un tiempito, pero recuerda: hay que aprender a freír despacio.

ANAMÚ: (*Algo más entusiasmada.*) Bueno, Milagritos, enséñanos algo.

MILLIE: Primero hay que conectarlo todo. (*Saca un enredo de cables de la caja.*)

ANAMÚ: ¿Y tú sabes donde va ese fracatán de cables?

MILLIE: Creo que sí ...

RUBÉN: (*Ayudando a Millie con los cables.*) A ver, te damos una manita ... Yo creo que aquí hay demasiados cables.

PEPE: Eso es fácil. Yo sé el Método Universal Para Armar y Conectar Todo Tipo de Aparato.

ANAMÚ: ¿Cómo es eso?

PEPE: Muy fácil ... usted verá ... (*Se da un trago de la botella. Recita lo que sigue de un tirón.*) Usted agarra el COSO con la mano izquierda. Con la derecha inserte el TURULETE en la COCLAÍNA, justo debajo de la CUCHUFLETA roja. Después, con mucho cuidado, le da una vuelta a la derecha hasta que oiga un click. Enseguidita atornille el SEMIÑOCO largo al CHIRIMBOLO amarillo. Ahora, muy importante, bajo ninguna circumstancia permita que el PERIFOLLO de metal haga contacto con la TIRITAÑA negra, si no, se le puede dañar el CACHIRULO, ¿entienden? ...

TODOS: No.

PEPE: No se preocupen. Vamos paso por paso . . .
GENO: Esperen . . . antes de empezar . . . (*Rocía Agua de Florida sobre la computadora.*)
MILLIE: Abuela, ¿qué haces? (*Seca con la mano el Agua de Florida.*)
GENO: Por si las moscas.
PEPE: Buena idea, Doña Geno. Hay que alejar los malos espíritus. (*Saca su hacha y la mueve sobre los aparatos.*) Estos aparatos son muy sensitivos a las malas vibraciones.
MILLIE: Vamos, vamos a conectar esto.
PEPE: Okay . . . agarre el coso con la mano derecha . . .
MILLIE: El coso con la mano derecha . . .
ANAMÚ: ¿Cuál coso?
CARMEN: (*Entra* CARMEN, *bien vestida y arreglada. No le hacen mucho caso.*) Hello, everybody! (*Nadie le responde. Va donde* RUBÉN y PEPE.) Hi, Rubén, how are you? And you, Mr. Indian?
RUBÉN: Nena, ¿tú hablando inglés?
CARMEN: Sí, estoy cogiendo clases por la noche.
RUBÉN: ¡Vaya!
PEPE: Justo debajo de la cuchufleta roja . . .
CARMEN: (CARMEN *toca a Doña Geno en el hombro.*) Hello, Doña Yeno. How do you do? Is me, Carmen!
GENO: ¡Mujer, casi ni te conozco!
CARMEN: Sí, gracias a sus recetas espirituales modernas . . .
GENO: ¿Recetas modernas?
CARMEN: Sí, la que me leyó Millie cuando usted estaba en el hospital . . . Me cambié el peinado, conseguí trabajo, me compré ropa nueva, estoy yendo a la escuela por la noche . . . y, no lo va a creer . . . ¡I have a boyfriend! (GENO *le echa una mirada a* MILLIE. MILLIE *se encoge de hombros.*)
PEPE: Rubén, atornilla el semiñoco largo . . . ¡no chico, ese es el chirimbolo!
RUBÉN: Perdone, chief.
ANAMÚ: (A CARMEN.) ¡Vaya! . . . ¿y quién es el dichoso?
CARMEN: No sé si lo conoces —se llama Arturo. ¡Ay, está enchuladísimo con mi pelo!
LUISA: (*Entrando apresuradamente.*) ¡Ay, que bueno que no han cerrado todavía! Doña Geno, necesito consultarle algo.
GENO: Ay, mi'jita, vas a tener que venir mañana. Ahora mi nieta va a hacer un "trabajito" aquí con este aparato . . . ¿Cuál es el problema? ¿Tu marido?

PEPE: ¡Cuidado! El perifollo de metal está rozando la tiritaña!
LUISA: No, ya eso se resolvió.
MILLIE: Rubén, ¡ten cuidado!
GENO: (*A* LUISA.) Yo sabía que las velas iban a trabajar ...
LUISA: No, no fueron las velas, Doña Geno.
GENO: ¿Qué fue entonces?
LUISA: Le dí una buena limpieza a la casa, hice un sahumerio, saqué toda la basura para afuera, puse la escoba detrás de la puerta y san se acabó!
GENO: ¿Qué pasó?
PEPE: ¡Que la tiritaña está mal enchufada!
LUISA: Boté a Arturo de la casa, con el resto de la basura.
MILLIE: Pásame la cuchufleta del input.
CARMEN: (*A* LUISA.) ¿Arturo? ¿Arturo es su marido?
LUISA: Era. Ya me despojé de ese mono que tenía en la espalda.
ANAMÚ: Fíjense bien, me parece que el semiñoco ese está flojo.
CARMEN: (*Para sí.*) ¡Ay virgen! (*A* DOÑA GENO.) Doña Geno ... tengo que hacerle una consulta ... a private consulta ...
GENO: Mañana, mañana ... ahora estoy ocupada ...
MILLIE: ¡Yo creo que ya está!
PEPE: Déjame chequearlo rapidito ... (*Tocando los cables rápidamente.*) Turulete, coclaína, semiñoco, chirimbolo, tiritaña, cachirulo. Sí, ya está.
RUBÉN: (*Enrollando cables y guardándolos en la caja.*) Yo dije que aquí iban a sobrar cables.
LUISA: (*Por primera vez se fija en la computadora.*) ¡Ay, pero qué tienen aquí! ¡Una tele! ¡Ahora puedo ver la novela aquí!
CARMEN: Excuse me, no es una tele. It is a computer.
GENO: Eso. La trajo Millie. Ahora nos va a hacer una demostración.
RUBÉN: Vamos, vamos, préndela.
ANAMÚ: Sí, sí, vamos. Estoy loca por ver para qué sirve un aparato como éste en una botánica.
MILLIE: Ya verán, ya verán.
CARMEN: (*Para sí, preocupada.*) Arturo ...
MILLIE: (MILLIE *se sienta ante la computadora. Los demás la rodean.*) Okay. Vamos a empezar con las yerbas. Abuela, tú me dices el nombre de la yerba y después para lo que se usa y yo lo voy a taipear aquí.
GENO: Hay tantas ... no sé por dónde empezar.
RUBÉN: Puede empezar por orden alfabético.
PEPE: Eso. En orden alfabético.

MILLIE: Si quieres, pero no es necesario. Se pueden poner en cualquier orden, porque después yo aprieto una de estas teclas y la máquina solita pone la lista en orden alfabético.
CARMEN: You should put them in English too.
MILLIE: Eso es otro paso. Primero vamos a ponerlas en español.
ANAMÚ: Espérate, no empieces todavía. Para sentirme más tranquila, déjame hacerle un rieguito antes de empezar.
MILLIE: Mamá, eso no hace falta . . .
ANAMÚ: Déjame . . . por si las moscas . . . (ANAMÚ *coge una botella de Agua de Florida y echa unas gotas alrededor y encima de la computadora. Se pasa por la cabeza y le unta en las manos a* MILLIE.)
MILLIE: Okay, ya podemos empezar. Dale abuela.
GENO: Bueno, pues . . . pon ahí . . . ¡Ay, no me hallo!
MILLIE: Come on, abuela!
RUBÉN: Doña Geno, no se me eche para atrás ahora.
ANAMÚ: Yo te puedo decir las que yo sé.
MILLIE: Okay, dale.
ANAMÚ: Yerba santa . . .
MILLIE: (*Tecleando.*) Yerba santa . . . ¿para qué sirve?

Apagón súbito. Reacciones de sorpresa de todos en la oscuridad.

LUISA: ¡Ay!
GENO: ¿Que pasó?
ANAMÚ: ¡Se fueron los tapones!
MILLIE: Shit!
PEPE: ¡Coño Rubén, te dije que tuvieras cuidado con la cuchufleta amarilla!
RUBÉN: Yo creo que es un blackout . . .
GENO: (*Escandalizada.*) Ya sabía yo que este embeleco no iba a ser del agrado de los santos . . .
CARMEN: (*Tropieza, se oye ruido.*) ¡Ay! Creo que me partí una canilla!
PEPE: Cuidado donde pisa, joven —eso era mi pie . . .
GENO: Anamú, enciende una vela, nos vamos a matar en esta boca de lobo . . . (ANAMÚ *enciende una vela,* RUBÉN *enciende otra.*)
MILLIE: Espero que no se me haya borrado toda la información . . .
GENO: ¿Tú quieres decir que si se va la electricidad, este aparato no funciona?
MILLIE: Claro que no . . .
GENO: ¿Y que todo lo que está ahí adentro se le puede olvidar?

MILLIE: Puede ser ...

GENO: ¡Valiente memoria esa! ¿De qué sirve si nada más recuerda cuando hay luz? A mí la memoria no me falla en la oscuridad ... te digo, no se puede depender de los aparatos ...

PEPE: A lo mejor me equivoqué —Rubén, chequea bien si el semiñoco rojo está conectado al turulete negro ...

RUBEN: A ver, aguanta aquí esta vela ...

ANAMÚ: Voy a chequear los tapones ... (*Sale.* RUBÉN *conecta y desconecta cables. Vuelve la luz. Reacciones y comentarios.*)

MILLIE: Vamos a ver si se borró algo ... (*Aprieta teclas. La pantalla se enciende de nuevo.*)

ANAMÚ: (*Entra* ANAMÚ.) ¿Qué pasó?

RUBÉN: Pues no sabemos ... (*A* MILLIE.) Is everything okay?

MILLIE: Parece que sí ... sí, aquí está ... Bueno, vamos a seguir, ¿por dónde íbamos?

GENO: No sé si vale la pena ...

ANAMÚ: Ay, mamá, todo el mundo usa estas cosas hoy en día ...

GENO: ¿Y si se van los tapones otra vez?

RUBÉN: Van a tener que cambiar los cables eléctricos ...

MILLIE: Forget it, abuela. A ver, íbamos por la yerba buena ...

ANAMÚ: Yerba santa.

CARMEN: Joli gras in inglis.

MILLIE: (*Tecleando.*) Yerba santa. ¿Para qué sirve eso?

GENO: Pa' la garganta.

MILLIE: (*Tecleando.*) Para la garganta. Okay, otra.

ANAMÚ: Abrecamino ...

GENO: Pa' su destino.

MILLIE: (*Tecleando.*) Abrecamino ... para el destino.

RUBÉN: Apasote ...

LUISA: Eso es para los frotes. (MILLIE *teclea.*)

ANAMÚ: También está la albahaca ...

CARMEN: Sí, esa es pa' la gente flaca ... for skinny people.

MILLIE: (*Tecleando.*) Albahaca ... para la gente flaca ...

PEPE: También está el vetiver para los que no ven ...

MILLIE: Hey, wait a minute! This sounds familiar ...

LOS DEMÁS: (*Cantando.*) ¡Y con esa yerba se casa usted!

MILLIE: ¡Se están burlando de mí!

GENO: No, m'ijita, no. Sigue, sigue.

ANAMÚ: Hija, taipea ... (*Cantando.*)

"Traigo yerba santa pa' la garganta

Traigo caisimón pa' la hinchazón
Traigo abrecamino pa' tu destino
Traigo la ruda pal que estornuda
También traigo albahaca pa' la gente flaca
el apasote para los frotes
el vetivé para el que no ve"

TODOS: ¡Y con esa yerba, se casa usted!»

CARMEN: (*Suena el teléfono.* CARMEN *corre a contestarlo.*) Ceiba Tree Boutique! May I help you ... yes, one moment please, who's calling? One moment ... (*Tapa el teléfono con la mano.*) Millie, is for you .... Mr. Ahabi. (MILLIE *no se mueve.* GENO, ANAMU y RUBÉN *la miran.* MILLIE *va al teléfono. Todos la siguen con la vista, expectativamente.* CARMEN *le pasa el teléfono. A* GENO.) ¿Quién es ese Ahabi?

GENO: Es el señor que quiere comprar el building ... (TODOS *siguen la conversación telefónica con gran interés.* RUBEN y GENO *casi aguantando la respiración.*)

MILLIE: Hello, Mr. Ahabi ... yes ... no, it won't be necessary because ... because I've changed my mind. No, it is not the money ... It's that ... my buffaloes are not for sale! ¿No comprende? I said no, ¡que mis búfalos no se venden!

GENO: ¡Un milagro!

(*Reacciones de júbilo de* RUBÉN *y* PEPE. GENO, ANAMÚ *y* MILLIE *se abrazan.*

Apagón.

En la oscuridad se escucha "El yerbero moderno" por Celia Cruz. Los actores salen a saludar con la canción de trasfondo. Después del último saludo de los actores, apagón. En la oscuridad se proyecta una diapositiva que es la foto de una computadora gigante. En la pantalla hay una imagen de Santa Bárbara en "computer design" guiñando un ojo.

Apagón final.

FIN